In the Arms of a Stranger

In the Arms of a Stranger

Stories from the Streets:
My Life as a Paramedic

Dale J Bingham

Writers Club Press
San Jose New York Lincoln Shanghai

In the Arms of a Stranger
Stories from the Streets: My Life as a Paramedic

Writers Club Press
an imprint of iUniverse, Inc.

For information address:
iUniverse, Inc.
5220 S. 16th St., Suite 200
Lincoln, NE 68512
www.iuniverse.com

ISBN: 0-595-20592-5

Printed in the United States of America

DEDICATION

This book is dedicated to all of those great partners and colleagues who I have worked with through the years; some who have become great friends and some that have disappeared into time. I thank you for your support and friendship as we worked through some of life's most difficult situations. I look at EMS as a great team. I know that I never did anything by myself and acknowledge that I was just a player on this team. I am grateful to have had this opportunity to serve others.

I also thank all those patients who taught me how to love and gave me some great memories. I wish I could have saved all those who wished to be saved, but I know that medicine is a Fickle beast; You never know why or why someone walks out of a car that now looks like an accordion and why the young innocent victim of a minor fender-bender never walks away at all. As much as we want to believe it or wish it, I know that the ultimate decision lies in the hands of a higher power whose time line is not always the same as ours. My colleagues and I are just tools in his hands.

Most importantly I thank my beautiful wife Lisa, who REALLY taught me how to love and let me come home from shift and just be myself. She never asked me about my runs or bad calls. I am so grateful for that because when I came home I needed to leave the day back there on the unit and start fresh. That's the only way I made it through.

I also thank my 4 beautiful children, Kourtney, Bryton, Bradley, and Kynzee. You are what I live for.

PREFACE

The Emergency Medical Services is a misunderstood and confusing entity. I have spent years trying to educate the public on its roles and responsibilities. I have tried to dispel myths and stereotypes about the men and women and the job they do. Nevertheless, many misconceptions still abound about what we do. I still have people ask me to this day, "Is someone going to ride in the back with the patient?" Many still believe that we drive up as fast as we can, grab the patient from the throngs of death and drive off to the hospital even faster than when we got there. TV often portrays EMS workers as a wild group of cold-hearted thrill seekers who always slam the emergency room doors open as they enter the hospital.

The sad reality is that we really do not save that many lives. Not because of poor care, but because people do not always call us out to save their lives. They call us out for the flu, for a hip fracture, or because they just lost their husband and just need someone to talk to, and sometimes we even to have to tell them that their loved one has passed on. We play the role of caregiver, of lifesaver, of psychologist, of grief counselor, and wear many, many, different hats. Sometimes I wonder if a better term for what we do is "life impacter" as opposed to "lifesaver". We impact a great many more lives than we save.

Training has expanded in recent years to become a true two-year program for those wishing to become paramedics. This is a largely misunderstood aspect of paramedicine. Schools are tough and demanding. The dropout and failure rate of paramedic programs tends to run very high. My own paramedic program began with over 30 students and I graduated with only 11. It is similar to the time to become a nurse yet specializes in emergency care as opposed to the long-term care focus of nursing. There are rotations in emergency care, obstetrics, pediatrics, psychiatric, and more. This doesn't include the on-the-job training required of all paramedics and EMS workers. It is both demanding and difficult.

If you think about it we must be just as ready at 3 AM as we do at 3 PM. We must be prepared to go a day without food, without sleep, without using the restroom if the situation so dictates. We must be just as prepared to deliver a newborn child as we do caring for a 100-year-old nursing home resident. We do care, we do cry, and we do hurt. We can get angry, frustrated, and fed up. But through it all we realize that we have a job to do and it has to get done. People are counting on us.

My first trainer's words still ring in my ears to this day. He said, "one must be past feeling and never, ever, get involved with our patient's pain and suffering. After all," he continued, "It's not our fault they got hurt." It took me about a day to realize that he was wrong. I have found over the years that those who give the best care are those who *are* the most caring and concerned for another's welfare. Still, it is a learning process. The initial thrill and draw of this career soon diminishes and is replaced by a greater feeling and emotion for the welfare of others, whether that means saving their life or uplifting their spirits.

I was recently asked by someone what I felt was the most important thing I've gotten out of being an EMS worker. I can answer truthfully that it is to just "love those you serve." Love them and serve them without regard to race, gender, economic status, or any other factor. Always remember that no one sets out to be an addict or alcoholic, or to get cancer, or to live homeless. True, there are consequences to some of our actions and many of these are amplified in emergency situations, but not one of us is perfect. No one needs to tell the mother whose child is in critical care now that the child should have been in a car seat. She knows—more than we know. No one needs to tell the emphysema patient that she shouldn't have smoked her whole life. She knows. Just love them and take care of them.

I hope this book reflects that love. I make no claims to perfection. I know that there are patients out there who were not pleased with my care. I have had and still have a lot of learning and growing up to do. But I know that I chose to be there for them, they didn't choose to be there for me. And to all those that I have had the opportunity to serve, I thank you for welcoming me into your homes, your cars, your workplace, and your lives. And I thank you for putting your trust in me—a total stranger.

LIST OF ABBREVIATIONS

Ambu-bag–Brand name of the bag-valve-mask. Used to breathe for a patient

Aneurysm–A dangerous bulging or bursting of an artery Most often the aorta, the largest artery in the body

Asystole–Commonly known as "flatline". The heart has stopped beating

Bretylium–A medication used to control rapid or fibrillating hearts

Backboard–A hard board that the patient lies on to help keep their back from moving

BVM–Bag Valve Mask. A device used to breathe for a patient

Cardiac Arrest–A patient's heart has stopped beating

C-Collar–A device put around the patient's neck to keep it still

C.I.S.D.–Critical incident stress debriefing

CPR–Cardiopulmonary resuscitation

Defibrillator–Device used to shock the heart

D.O.–Doctor of Osteopathy

D.O.A.–Dead on Arrival

EKG–Electrocardiogram. Used to check the rhythm of the heart

EMT–Emergency Medical Technician

EMS—Emergency Medical Service

EMSA—Emergency Medical Service Authority

ER–Emergency room

ETA–Estimated time of arrival

Hemothorax–Blood in the lung cavity

Intubation–The process of putting a breathing tube down a patient's throat

IV–Intravenous. A line put into a vein to pass fluid and medications

Lidocaine–A medication used to treat rapid or fibrillating hearts

Lifelight–One of the medical helicopter services serving the Tulsa metropolitan area

PD–Police department

PEA–Pulseless electrical activity. A condition in which the heart appears to have a rhythm on the ECG, but no heartbeat is present

Porthole–Term used to describe the window located between the cab to the back of an ambulance.

Post–Some EMS systems work a 12, rather than 24-hour shift. Usually these services put their units at strategic locations throughout their response area. These locations are called "posts"

VA–Veterans administration

INTRODUCTION

I never really thought that I would have a career as a paramedic. It just sort of happened that way. To this day I can still remember sitting next to one of my classmates in our history class at Millikan High School and listening to the "war stories" of his weekend ride alongs with a local ambulance service. We were both seniors in high school, but he had already taken an off-campus class that trained him to become an emergency medical technician. Unfortunately for him he was not able to find work until he graduated. So he would ride along voluntarily on the weekends and then come to class on Monday with what seemed to me like a million and one stories about the "mean streets" of Orange County, California. I admit that the stories were interesting, but blood and guts were not my thing. So I remember telling him that, "I could never do that–I can't handle the blood."

I have since learned to never say never.

After graduation I made an attempt at college, but since I couldn't figure out the paperwork I decided to just go to work for awhile. So I worked in a facility that housed the developmentally disabled. I remember watching the ambulance personnel come in for emergencies and thought that they were "cool". But I really didn't give it much thought until my father, who had taken an EMT class, suggested I look into a regional occupations program there in Orange County. I told him the same thing I told my friend in school; "I can't handle the blood." But in reality I wanted to do something fulfilling and rewarding. That and the occupational program there was free. I really liked that part of it.

So I reluctantly enrolled.

The rest for me is my own history.

I received an "A" in the class and that made me fell much better about doing it. I also realized that the "blood and guts" that I was so afraid of, was in reality such a minor part of what EMS workers do. It is so much more about caring and giving. About helping others mentally and emotionally as much as it is about saving lives. It is and it isn't the Emergency! Series that we saw on television.

The first company I applied at after getting my license was Schaffers Ambulance in Costa Mesa. Schaffers was the service they always showed on the Emergency! Television series so I thought that they had to be a good service. I went in and took some type of bizarre written test and then had an interview with three men. I didn't know it at the time, but the written test did not go very well. In the interview they asked me some questions about subjects I had never learned about and had a few laughs after some of my answers. I was very uneasy and thought that they were very unprofessional. Today I realize that they were actually making fun of me. I was very young and naïve at the time so I did not realize it immediately. Nevertheless they let me know I was not going to be hired.

Dejected after that interview, I went over to Southland Ambulance in Anaheim. I didn't go there at first because many people had told me that they had a "terrible reputation". They never told me why, just that I shouldn't go there. But I wanted to work and I felt that given the experience of my interview at Schaffers, I couldn't be picky.

I walked in the door at Southland Ambulance, filled out an application, and was immediately called back to a room for an interview. I was very nervous, having my earlier interview on my mind, and hoping I would be able to answer the questions right. But "Mike", was wonderful. He asked a few questions that were generic in nature and then asked if I could start the next week. I about fell off of my chair. I remember fumbling for some words and then telling him *I* would like to give my current job two weeks notice. He said fine, told me to show up in two weeks, shook my hand, and then led me out of the room. It was that easy.

And I had my first EMS job.

I have worked for a number of services in three different states over the years, but Southland was the first. It is where my roots will always be. You could say it was kind of like a first love–I'm glad they were there, but I am also glad I moved on.

During my career I have also taken a few stops here and there for education. I feel that education is invaluable and almost a necessity if one wants to feed a family someday. I got through one of the toughest paramedic programs in LA County, earned an associate degree from the front of an EMSA ambulance while taking telecourses and independent study courses, and then earned a BS in Health Services to complement my career in EMS. As time and a career wore on me I became a "part-time" paramedic and took a full-time position teaching EMS at Rogers State University in Oklahoma.

I must say here that, in my professional opinion, there is a profound difference between those who work for a public agency, meaning a fire department, and those who work for a private EMS service, whose sole purpose is to generate a profit. I have been a private sector worker my entire career, although the Emergency Medical Service Authority (EMSA) in Tulsa had the elements of both. It is a different world in the private sector. For starters the pay is notoriously low. I started out at Southland Ambulance at $4.06 in the mid 1980's, went to Adams Ambulance for $3.35 and hour after that and my top pay as a paramedic on the streets has been $11.60 per hour.

The hours were long too. At Southland I worked 4—12 hour shifts on with 2 days off in a rotation. That may not seem like much to some, but in a career like this it takes a toll very quickly. Some days you were lucky to get a break long enough to go to the bathroom. At Adams Ambulance I worked an A/B schedule, meaning I was on B shift and I worked every Tuesday, Thursday, and Saturday for a 24-hour shift. Every other weekend I was required to work a double and that was only if you were lucky enough during the week not to get "mandatory holdover". If you think of it, I only got 2 days off in a row twice a month–if I didn't get held over for another 24-hour shift (which was very common). At the time I was single and could do it, but once marriage came I could no longer do it without being greatly distressed for my time and energy. Marriage and EMS is often a volatile mix. It worked for me, but I have seen hundreds of others who it didn't work for. For many, they live and breathe EMS and forget about the things in life that matter most to their own well being. For me, without my beautiful wife Lisa I would have never made it. She has always realized that home is home for me and work needs to stay at work. She always has let me leave it there. I am eternally grateful for that. I needed that.

I went from Adams to Care Ambulance in Anaheim, California. They were primarily a transfer service that was family owned, but they absolutely knew how to treat their employees. To this day I feel that I could work for the Richardson family any time. It was and has been my favorite place to work, even though they were not a first response agency at the time. Since the time I worked there I have periodically stopped in at Care to see how they have done over the years. Every time I stop by they have grown bigger and better, even in these tough economic times. I am happy that the "good guys always win."

From there I found myself in Provo, Utah, working for Valley Ambulance Service. I was only there a short while when paramedic school came calling back in California. We packed it in and moved again. I went to Mount San Antonio College in Walnut, California. It had a tremendous reputation of being the hardest and most difficult program in Southern California. I admit it was tough, but I was up to the challenge. Thirty something students started and eleven graduated. I was grateful to be one of the eleven.

From there my family took a brave leap and my wife, my daughter Kourtney, my in vitro son, Bryton (Due in 6 months), and of course, myself took a job offer in Tulsa, Oklahoma, working for the Emergency Medical Service Authority. It was the best thing we ever did as a family. EMSA was and is an extremely progressive EMS agency. As the only paramedic on the ambulance there is a very heavy responsibility that weighs on upon one's shoulders. It was demanding, but rewarding. The experience gained there was and is invaluable today. While I only find myself working part-time as a street paramedic (I consider myself semi-retired) I sometimes miss the adrenaline rush that used to come with the job. Every once in a while I feel it on some run, somewhere, but not like when I was younger. Instead, I cherish the opportunity to help others survive in a career like this. That is why I teach now. I think I will always be involved in EMS somehow and someway, even when I am old and gray. I may be like my own father, who listens to his scanner from his recliner and monitors the EMS runs. No matter what I believe it is something that gets into your blood and never leaves.

By the way, I still do not like the blood and guts. But I love helping others…and that makes it all worth while.

CONTENTS

~ DAY ONE ~

Well, here I was, first day. I remember they put me with some lady whose name I can't remember today, even if you offered me a million dollars to remember it. I remember her personality well, just not the name. She was rough, crude, and rude, and at this point in my career I can look back and understand why she didn't have a partner that day—though I think I caught on about midway through the shift, when she lied and told dispatch that we were about a mile and a half closer than we really were to an emergency. She told me at the time that, "She could get there just as fast as any one else could."

I realized that that was not a good quality.

I don't really know what I expected that first day, but I remember being nervous. I had done only one ambulance ride as part of my EMT class and that day I rode we only had one transfer call–we didn't even turn on the siren. For my orientation at Southland Ambulance they had me ride as a third rider for one shift. We didn't turn on the sirens that day either, but to Southland that was orientation–one shift as a third man on a crew. I learned nothing on that one orientation day, except that I learned that orientation was a joke. So needless to say, my first day I felt absolutely clueless. The one expectation I did have for the first day was that we had to at least turn on the siren.

We would. About midway through the hot Southern California afternoon the first "real" emergency came our way. It was a cardiac arrest at the Anaheim Lakes fishing area. I can't really describe what it is like to race through Southern California traffic for the first time with lights and sirens blaring–especially with this lady driving–but I think I must have worn the biggest Gomer Pyle grin on my face that any one has ever seen. I will never forget that feeling.

I remember pulling up to the scene and seeing a blue, older model, pickup parked near the lake and next to a tree with it's driver side door open. That was my first impression. On the ground nearby the Anaheim firemen and paramedics were doing CPR on an older Hispanic man. I think that was the first time that I actually saw anyone doing CPR in person and up close. All I had seen up to that point was on video. He lay there with his shirt wide open, his body not moving. He was obviously lifeless. I walked up with the gurney and tried to follow my partners cue, after all, I had no idea what I was supposed to be doing. She looked over a fireman's shoulder and, calling him by name, asked if there was anything she could do.

Then my nightmare began.

I stood there trying to watch, and learn I guess, when that same fireman who she had called by first name, pointed straight at me and told me firmly, "Get some more O2 off of the firetruck. We are running out!" That was during the time we used the positive pressure-breathing device for all arrests instead of a bag-valve-mask. Unfortunately, they had a tendency to deplete the tank of oxygen quickly. I had enough sense to ask in a panic, "where are they?"

He mumbled something to the effect of, "Blah, blah, blah." And pointed toward the two brand new Emergency One firetrucks parked about 30 yards away. I didn't understand exactly what he said, but I did think to myself that a big green oxygen tank couldn't be that hard to find…at least it shouldn't be that hard.

But it was.

I searched everywhere on those two trucks, in the compartments on the outside, up on the hose bed, even in the enclosed passenger compartments. I ran back to scene. The fireman at the head looked up again and asked, "Where is the damn oxygen?"

I explained my case to him as fast as I could. He told me again, in no uncertain terms, where the oxygen was located. All I heard again was "Blah, blah, blah." But I ran back to the trucks like a good little EMT. I looked high and low, frontways, sideways, underneath, but no oxygen. I was panicked on the inside, almost ready to cry. But I knew I had to go back and face the wrath of a scorned firefighter. I didn't know it at the time, but to the majority of firemen in Orange County the ambulance EMT's were not part of "the team", but were there for the paramedics grunt work and transport. The majority made sure to remind us of that daily. Many times they would meet us at the door of a house where an emergency was and ask us to "wait outside until they call us in to pick up the patient."

I went back, scared out of my head to face them, and of course the fireman at the head of the patient hollered, cussed, called me stupid, you name it, until another paramedic told me to take over chest compressions and that he would go get the oxygen bottle. I took over compressions in the hot California sun and they never let me relinquish them for the next 30 minutes. I had to do them on scene, to the ambulance, and enroute to the hospital. At one point, covered in sweat and my arms cramping, I voiced up and told them I was getting tired. I remember one of them telling me that they didn't have any one at the moment who could replace me. Yea right. Payback.

We took the man to Canyon General hospital. On the way to the hospital I remember thinking to myself that I didn't like this job very much and I wasn't too sure there would be a shift number two. Our patient was pronounced dead shortly after we arrived at the ER. It was my first death in the field and wouldn't be my last. Yet at the time I somehow, naively, thought everyone was saved. After all, that was our job–to save people. But I learned otherwise that day. I also thought that "lifesavers" were always nice to others. I was wrong both times.

~ WRESTLEMANIA~

My Second day was much better than the first. I was put with Phil. Phil had a boom box in the porthole window (the area between the cab and the patient compartment), a HUGE scissors pack on his belt, his own scanner, and experience. To a young teenage EMT–he was Joe cool. But more than that he was nice and friendly. It appeared that he got along with everybody. I needed that after the first day.

I only remember only one run from that day. I could never forget it. It was late in the shift when we were responded to a call in Buena Park. Buena Park was primarily my hometown, I had spent most of my growing up there, and it just felt good to respond there. I bet it felt good because it was one thing in this business I actually knew about. I have to admit that I was pretty clueless at this point in my young career, as this call would so clearly demonstrate.

I remember passing over the scene on the highway. I looked down to my right as we passed over on our way to the off ramp and looked into the backyard of a house that bordered the highway. I saw the Buena Park Fire Department and Police Department on the scene already talking to a man who sat on the ground in backyard of the house. Everything looked calm to me.

We pulled off and around to the house. A Buena Park fireman met us as we entered the yard. "He is having flashbacks. He's a Vietnam vet and wants to get some help," he reported to us, "He wants to go over to the VA in Long Beach."

Phil shook his head in the affirmative. I copied with my own weak nod.

"Oh yea," the fireman told us in an afterthought, "he's calm. Shouldn't have any problems."

Phil asked if he was on a hold. The fireman told him no, and that he was going "voluntarily."

I have learned over the years that voluntarily often means; "*You can either go with the ambulance or go to jail. You pick.*" It's a great trick of the police officers to avoid a report.

Anyway I was in no position to negotiate. Phil told me that we could just walk the patient over to the ambulance and have him sit on the bench seat. Easy enough for me, I thought. But once we stood the man up I noticed his height and stature. He was huge and very threatening looking. And the long Grizzly Adams beard didn't help much. He reminded me of a lumberjack who should be hauling logs north of Seattle.

But he seemed calm. When we told him to sit on the bench he complied with no problem. He allowed us to fasten his seatbelt without any complaint. Since I was new I wasn't trained to drive the unit yet, so I *had* to be in the back with him. But that was all right with me as patient care was what I was in this for. Yep, I was a lifesaver. It was my job to see to it that we got there safely. And it was a job I took very seriously.

Too seriously.

Phil peeked through the porthole, "You alright?' he asked, "We should be there in a few."

I nodded to him that I was fine. He nodded back and slammed the porthole window shut while turning up his boombox. And then we drove off.

As we started down the 405 I turned to my patient to make small talk. "Are you doing OK," I asked.

"Yup," came the reply. He looked straight at the floor.

"What's your name?"

He didn't answer.

"Sir," what's your name?" I asked again.

Again he didn't answer. Instead he started to unbuckle his seatbelt.

"Uhm, sir," I said, my voice beginning to crack, "You need to keep that on."

He scooted toward the side door, never looking at me. "We need to get out," he said. "They're coming."

"It's OK," I reassured him. "Who's coming?"

"They're right out there!" He started making machine gun sounds and formed his hands as if he was shooting out the window. "The Cong. We have to get out."

He reached for the door handle. "Sir," I said firmly, but with some crackling, "It's OK. Get away from the door. I reached for his arm.

He jerked it back. "Who are you?" He asked. "You're one of them," he said glaring at me.

I thought fast. "No, no I am with you."

"Your one of them!"

"No, I am with you. On your side," I tried to convince him "Don't bail out they will get you."

"We have to get out!" he hollered again.

By this point I was getting frustrated and scared. I looked down as he leaned back toward the door and saw a knife in his boot. I made up my mind that that knife would not come out. No way would that knife come out. I glanced up through the porthole window toward the driver's seat. Phil was driving along tapping his hand to the music while I wrestled Grizzly Adams in the back.

But it was *my* responsibility to take care of the patient in the back and Grizzly was my patient.

"Can't you see them shooting?" he yelled. "We have to jump out."

I hollered back again, "Don't jump, they'll get us." This time he slid back across the bench to the back door. I heard the handle click. Thinking fast (panic will do that to you) I dove for him from my spot on the gurney. I grabbed him hard. He pushed all 150 pounds of me back. I came at him again as he opened the door slightly. "I've got to get out of here!" he yelled.

I saw the flash of the boot knife again. He hadn't reached for it, but I didn't want him to either. I became determined that I would win this battle. I grabbed him with one arm while pulling the door shut with the other. We tumbled onto the gurney and halfway onto the floor. I put him in a headlock and held on for dear life. He struggled for a moment, then relaxed a little. Thank heavens this is one of those times that the patient had a little alcohol in his system.

He calmed down and I released my death grip. He scooted back to the bench.

"It's gonna be alright," I reassured him, knowing full well that if he wanted to he could probably crush me with one hand.

He looked back down at the floor. He didn't say a word.

About that time Phil opened the back door. "We're gonna probably need security," I told him. Phil looked up at me, my hair frazzled, my uniform untucked, and probably the terrified look in my eyes, and asked, "What happened?"

I rehearsed the situation too him and told him of my epic David versus Goliath battle on the 405. Somehow I was a little proud. I had kept him in the unit and got him to the hospital, albeit with a few scrapes and bruises.

Phil looked at me with a quizzical look in his eyes. "Why didn't you just tell me. He's not on a hold. He could have hurt you" Then he smirked, "All we had to do was pull over and let him out. Then we could call PD."

Uhm, yea, I knew that. Thanks for telling me, Phil.

~ CLOSEST CALL ~

I had two partners for my first permanent shift. It was split into 2-day segments and on the first two days of the shift my partner was Wes, an "old timer" of about 5 years, and the second two days I worked with Steve. Wes was decent usually, but had a hot temper. I felt as if I could never do anything fast enough. On many occasions, if he felt that I did not push the gurney fast enough for him, he would yank it out of my hands. He wouldn't say anything, just pull it out of my hands. At least he did know the business and I learned a lot watching him. Oh yea, he also had a large boom box that he brought with him every shift, since Southland refused to put FM radios in the units. He liked to listen to the rock station KLOS...so he did have some good qualities.

Steve, on the other hand, was funny, easy going, and helpful. He was older than me by quite a few years, married, and he knew the business. He put people at ease, myself included. I was with Steve on this particular night.

We responded to a seedy hotel on Katella avenue, directly across the street from the world famous Disneyland. These hotels/motels had a tendency to attract a great deal of heroin addicts and other assorted characters. The call came in as a possible cardiac arrest involving a child and somehow we managed to beat the Anaheim Fire Department to the scene. I remember walking up to the hotel room, which faced the parking lot. The first thing I noticed was two adult men meeting us at the door.

"I don't think she's breathing," one of them told us. They were in shorts with no shirts. I glanced around the two men and into the dimly lit room. I could see a little bundle of something lying on the bed; it turned out to be the baby, near the door. Other children of varying ages were also in the room, some of them crying and screaming, a few of them watching TV.

"What happened?" Steve asked as we entered the room.

"We found her in the playpen like this when we checked on her," one of the men said with a strange calmness. The smell of alcohol permeated the room.

Steve reached down and checked the baby's pulse. I watched for any rise and fall of the chest, but saw nothing. I looked at Steve with a "What the heck are we supposed to do now?" look, after all, I didn't learn about babies in EMT class. Thankfully, he must have read my mind because he looked up and said, "We are going to have to breathe for the baby."

I hesitated for a moment. I am not sure why, I think I was just nervous. I knew what to do, but I just didn't do it–or couldn't do it. Steve hesitated too, but I believe he hesitated for a reason–he wanted me to do mouth to mouth. But when I didn't move quickly enough he grabbed the baby and started breathing for her. That was the difference between Steve and Wes; Wes would have told me to do it while Steve just did it. Not that Wes didn't care, but he truly acted more the "senior" medic and had no problem telling me what to do. Steve breathed and did chest compressions on the little baby until fire came crashing through the door.

Thank heavens, that is the closest in my career I have ever come to doing mouth to mouth–on duty or off.

After Anaheim Fire arrived we transported the baby to Western Medical Center–Anaheim. They couldn't save her. In hindsight I realize now that the baby was stiff and cold. She'd died long before we got there. But strangely, there was more to the story.

Somehow there always is.

After we had brought the baby in we stood outside the ER cleaning our unit up. An Anaheim police officer came up to us and asked for a statement from both Steve and myself. We told him what we saw and heard at the scene. Steve, the veteran, asked the officer why he wanted to know and if something was wrong with our care. The officer then told us that they found bite marks and bruises on the baby. Not little kid bite marks, but adult bite marks.

Some adult had bitten the baby.

We hadn't seen or looked for anything like that in the dimly lit hotel room, but once again in my naivete, I didn't think I needed to.

~ STOP AND GO ~

Steve and I sat on our Anaheim post at the corner of Harbor and Banner Street. We were talking, drinking some pop, and basically just resting until the next call came in. As we sat there baked up against the brick wall at the back of the AM/PM convenience store parking lot, a car full of Hispanic males blazed past us in their older model four door car and then out into the street.

Normally, I wouldn't notice anything unusual about something like that, after all, it was Southern California, but something was different about these guys. They stared at us as they went by. I could have sworn they looked right into our eyes. Being the good medic I was I politely waved to them and then went back to talking and drinking my pop. They didn't wave back.

We would soon find out why.

A minute or two after the car passed by us some bystanders drove up and told us that there was someone hit by a car right in front of us, at the edge of the parking lot. I didn't see anyone get hit by a car, Steve didn't see anyone get hit by a car, and neither of us heard any skid.

But someone was hit by a car.

Craning our necks we could see a moped and a person down right in front of us at the edge of the parking lot, about 40 yards away. The spot where we had parked was in a recess, so unless we really stood up to see, we couldn't see the scene. That is why we didn't see it happen. Our friends who blazed past us in the parking lot had seen it. They had caused it, but they were not sticking around to find out what happened.

We quickly let dispatch know that we had a serious accident and drove over to the patient. He was a young teenage boy who lay in the gutter. Next to him lay the remains of a moped. Neither was moving.

Steve, much more the veteran than I was, quickly assessed the patient as we waited for the Garden Grove Fire Department paramedics to arrive. The patient lay in the gutter not moving and breathing very heavy and slow. Steve told me that we had a serious head injury patient on our hands. I looked down and could see some blood coming from one of his ears. Steve told me that that is often a very bad sign. He took out a white 4x4 gauze pad and did the "halo test" to see if the patient was leaking spinal fluid, a very ominous sign. It was the only time in my whole career I have ever seen anyone do that particular test. We didn't see a positive "halo".

The patient was breathing heavy so we put him on high flow oxygen. We kept his head as still as we could. And then we held on.

The paramedics arrived and we packaged the young boy up as careful as we could. There was no way to tell what kind of injuries he might have had. It was obvious he was in critical condition. We took him over to University of Irvine Medical Center. He never did regain consciousness during the transport, but he survived the accident.

The men who hit him were long gone by the time the police department arrived.

But at least I was nice enough to have waved to them.

~ BIRDS OF A FEATHER ~

"Get this jacket off!" the Anaheim Fire captain yelled to me, "Do it quick!"

We stood in the tiny street just off of Anaheim Boulevard, working feverishly to save the life of the unconscious motorcycle rider who lay in the middle of the street. I was the one given the assignment to get the jacket off and never had I been so anxious to use my new trauma shears. They glistened in the morning sun as I brandished them like a true professional, cutting, snipping, and tearing at the thick jacket. The real thick jacket.

The down jacket.

While the weather was cool that morning it was also windy, and a brisk breeze blew between the buildings on the tiny, slim, street we were on. One fireman controlled the airway, one controlled c-spine, and others, along with my partner readied the backboard and c-collar. And I kept on cutting.

Now I'd never owned a down jacket. And I definitely didn't know that they were full of feathers, but they are. Lots of feathers. As I cut they began to come out little by little, then more and more. Pretty soon the whole scene looked like an episode of the old keystone cops movies, where they all ran around covered in feathers and throwing pies at each other. All we needed was the pie.

Feathers were every where. One of the paramedics looked at me and asked, with a perplexed look on his face, "What are you doing?"

Making a mess that's what. If we were in the military I could have yelled out, "FOLLOWING ORDERS, SIR!" But we weren't and I didn't. I just said, "Uh?"

And he said, "Stop cutting!"
And I said, "Ok."
And I think he said, "Idiot."

~ CHOICES ~

We responded to another motel on the "Disneyland" strip. Michael was my new partner and for the first time in my life I was working a night shift. I didn't do nights well then and I still don't do night shifts well. But I was young then and thought I'd give it a try.

It was early in the evening when Mike and I got this call. Troy was on the radio dispatching. Everyone liked Troy, as he seemed to look out for the crews and had a very upbeat and almost crazy personality. What many of us would come to find out was that Troy had a very serious drug addiction and his life would take a different turn later on. I believe he was a truly nice guy, but much of his peppiness came from something else. But this night he was on the radio. I remember him giving us the call as we drove to post. He told us that we had a "gunshot victim" at the motel. The adrenaline instantly flowed with those magic words. I remember him telling us that we had a police officer on scene and that it was safe to go in.

So we barreled down Katella Avenue, lights and sirens blaring, and pulled into the hotel parking area. Unfortunately, (or fortunately if you liked the excitement and really wanted to do something with your skills) we beat fire there again.

The hotel was an open hotel, meaning all the doors faced the outside. It was also shaped like a square so that all the rooms were readily visible to us. There was only one way in and one way out. We pulled right into the middle and got out of the unit. Mike was driving on that run so it took him a few seconds to get around the unit. Some anxious bystanders, on the other hand, instantly cornered me. They told me that someone was shot in one of the rooms upstairs. They pointed to a room on the second floor. A few bystanders were also on the stairs and on the balcony. They

15

hollered to me that a lady had been shot. I asked them who did it, but they said they didn't know. They just kept screaming for me to get up there.

Now I knew the rules about scene safety and I definitely valued my life, but for some reason I felt compelled to go up the stairs. I think that it was just the pressure from the bystanders urging and begging. Nevertheless, I climbed the stairs slowly, nervously, and I am ashamed to say, somewhat excited. I am sure it was just the rush of adrenaline, but there was a certain daring thrill to it.

The 3 bystanders stood about four to five doors down from the victim's room. Mike, as he did to me many times, found a way to make me do the dirty work. He said that he would "wait for fire and tell them what room."

Yea, thanks Mike.

By the way, did I mention that there was no police officer on the scene. We had been given wrong information. I am guessing on purpose, as Troy liked to see us get some "action". Either way, I was on my own.

I inched my way up the stairs and along the wall toward the hotel room. A couple of times I wanted to back down and wait, but the pressure from the bystanders to "do something" was almost unbearable. They kept hollering at me as if really wanting to say, "Hey idiot, get up there and help this lady. That's your job!" They knew nothing about scene safety.

The door to the victim's room was open slightly, and peering around the corner of the room I saw that it was dark except for a little light coming from the bathroom door at the far end of the motel room. I swear I saw the bathroom door swinging, but it may have just been my imagination. I guess I should have turned and ran and maybe I wanted to, but instead I hollered out the first thing that came to mind, "Hello?"

Suddenly a voiced moaned pitifully, "I'm right here."

I jumped back and looking down at where the voice came from I saw her. A middle aged woman on all fours right next to the open door. In my excitement I didn't see her at first, but now she lay at my feet. I screamed to her, "Where's the gun?" That was the only thought that came to mind at that instant.

But she didn't answer.

"Where is the gun, Lady?" I asked louder, as if she couldn't hear me.

"It's in there," she mumbled.

"In where?" I asked, "Who shot you?"

"No one," she said. "The gun is in there."

I didn't quite know what she meant, but in my stupidity I stepped over her and into the dark room. At this point all I could think about was where that gun was. I don't know why. It wasn't something I had learned or been taught, but in my mind I had to know the gun was secure. At this point it seemed like an eternity already, and yet no fire department was on scene.

I stood there and looked around the room. I didn't see anyone else or a gun. I got firm this time,

"Lady, where is the gun?"

I thought I heard her say, "on the bed." So I looked among the bloody and wrinkled sheets and indeed, there among the sheets on the bed, lay the pistol. The gun was now secure.

I now went back to what I was trained to do and knelt down next to the lady. She still sat there on all fours, obviously struggling for breath. She didn't say much to me. I noticed that she had some blood on her chest.

Just about that point the Anaheim paramedics walked in, never too soon for me, and laid her to her back. One of them quickly cut the lady's shirt open. When he did, a piece of metal fell from the bra. I remember him commenting that he thought that was very strange to see this piece fall out. It turned out that this was a bullet fragment from the 22 bullet hitting her rib and fragmenting. She had shot herself in the chest in an unsuccessful suicide attempt.

When I went down to help Mike get the gurney, the captain of engine 3 caught me and asked me what I was doing up there when PD was not there yet. I tried explaining that I couldn't exactly explain what I was doing up there, but to no avail, he proceeded to lecture me on the dangers of going up there and that it was not my place to go in first. And he said that he should call our boss and report me. He didn't, but I didn't really care if he did since I didn't really know why I had done what I did. I learned then that sometimes we do things without exactly knowing why we do them, as if someone is always looking over our shoulders. I know I didn't practice good scene safety on that run, but my intentions were good. And I don't know, maybe every EMS worker has their own angel watching over them.

I do know that we need one.

~ Smile as You Go Down ~

Mike and I were approaching the end of our night shift with only had an hour and a half to go. We both lay in the back of the ambulance at our post, Harbor Boulevard and Banner Street, Mike on the bench seat and I on the gurney, trying to catch a few winks. We did that often since we didn't have a station. We just sat at some street corner in a certain part of town until an emergency came in. Hey, you learn to adapt in this business.

Suddenly the tones of the Anaheim Fire Department broke the night silence. Mike reached up and turned up his Radio Shack scanner. *Beep, beep, beep; aunk, beep, aunk,* and the tones continued on until we recognized it as the customary tones for a 'heavy rescue'. We sat up listening intently as the Fire Department dispatcher sent the fire units to a motor vehicle accident with possible heavy rescue involved–and it was in our response area!

So we jumped into the front and waited for our dispatch to send us that way. There was always a lag between the fire dispatch and ours and the wait seemed like an eternity. But our dispatcher finally sent us to the call. And so we barreled down the road waking up the neighborhood at six-o'clock on a Sunday morning. We arrived to find the fire department already on scene. They hadn't been there for long as they were still pulling equipment off of the truck.

We jumped out and ran over to the vehicle. It was a white pickup truck that had slammed into a telephone pole. The front end had been smashed into the cab. A body was in the front seat, on the driver's side, slumped over to the left and pinned in the dash. I also noticed as we approached the truck (we had parked behind it) that the license plate had printed around the rim "Smile as you go down". Anaheim Fire worked like crazy

19

to free the trapped man inside the wreckage. He was not smiling. He was not moving or breathing either that I could tell. The 'Jaws of Life' had to be used to finally free him from the smashed pickup. We drug him out onto a backboard and laid him to the ground. The intubation equipment and the Ambu-bag were ready to go. The lead paramedic said that "he," the patient, "was still warm and we are going to have to work him."

I got in position, ready to do whatever they asked, when the other paramedics all consulted and decided that this patient was deceased. They pronounced him dead then and there. A suicide note was found in the truck telling us how distraught this young man was over some girl who was probably home sleeping peacefully. I couldn't believe he'd drove into the pole on purpose. To this day I hate running on suicides. There is definitely something otherworldly in the air at a suicide and they give me the creeps.

A few seconds later one of the firemen hollered out, "Hey look over here!" as he stood on the passenger side of the truck. We all naturally ran over there to look. And there, to all of our surprise, painted on the wrinkled and smashed side of the truck, in black spray paint, was the word OUCH!

That someone had painted on after the accident, before any of us arrived.

~ My Own Nightmare ~

Working in your own town has its benefits, but it also carries the possibility that you may run on someone you know. I had heard stories about that. One partner told of how a friend of his ran on his girlfriend in a car accident. Another told me the story of how one of the firemen responded to a fatality accident to find that it was his own son.

When you're young and naïve, you take these stories in, but the feelings at age 19 are not the same feelings as those when you get older. Life is something to be lived at age 19, not something to live for, and I was in the midst of living.

Surviving on $4.00 an hour you could say.

But I was in heaven here. I'd made something of myself. I was helping others and felt important. Not too many people get to experience the feeling or the excitement of a job like mine. While I was limited as an EMT basic in the things I could do, and even more limited by the company I worked for, there was still that aura about EMS that is unexplainable.

On this shift I recall it being very busy. This is somewhat of a misnomer as my experience in the business, with a few different companies, has taught me that system status management (posting units at strategic locations around the response area) is always busy. Today though, I found myself posted at corporate headquarters, aptly named "corporate", and standing next to a friend of mine, dispatcher Pete Morales. I watched over his shoulder as he took calls on the antiquated dispatch system. Even then, 1987, it was not computerized yet. I watched as the call would come in and then Pete would move the little cardboard ambulance across the large map of Orange County to signify that unit's status. At this particular moment I watched him as he took a call from the Buena Park Fire

21

Department. This is where I spent most of my childhood and where I was living with my parents at the time. Still I didn't think anything of it until Pete repeated back the address to the other dispatcher across the phone line.

"10-4, 6502 Christine Circle. We'll get a unit on the way."

I turned completely pale at that moment. I recognized the address. 6502 Christine Circle. MY HOUSE!

Before Pete could give me the call I told him, "I can't take that call Pete. That's my house."

"You're all I have," he replied, "There is no one else."

"Please Pete," I begged, pleaded, "send someone else."

Pete had been a good friend from the time I started. I could tell he wanted to help.

"What is it?" I asked, knowing it was probably something to do with my mother, who had a severe addiction to prescription drugs. Yet part of me was worried that it was far worse. After all, I still had 5 sisters and 2 brothers at home.

"Overdose," He said.

Mom.

I saw Pete shuffling around, calling units, checking on their status. And then finally! A unit nearby became available. Pete sent them instead of us, but he let my partner and I drive over to my house to see what was going on. I had no idea what to expect. This wasn't the first time she'd done something like this. This took a few minutes and the other unit had already pulled away when we got to my house. We went to Anaheim General to check on her status, and while it was a very critical overdose, requiring some time in ICU, she turned out all right. For now.

The future would have different plans for my mother.

This hit home. Scared me. While I managed to wiggle my way out of being the primary caregiver and responding unit, I still know that I was the first unit sent to my own home. I admit I didn't like the feeling in the least. A short time later I decided to go to work in LA County and get away from the place where I grew up.

I needed to. I had to.

~ ANOTHER TOMORROW ~

Twenty is a tough age. We find ourselves in a perilous transition from the far edge of puberty to the brink of adulthood. We know it all, but yet we know so little. I was twenty in the mid eighties. Disco was gone, rap wasn't quite here yet, and angst was never even heard of outside of a thesaurus. Reagan owned the decade. I owned very little.

And there was A.I.D.S.

AIDS was still new, threatening, misunderstood. Just the word sparked fear in many, myself included.

At the time I working for Adams Ambulance service in the city of Southgate, California. I was young, naive, eager, and still ready to take on the world. And I feared AIDS. Not necessarily that I'd "catch" it (I didn't), but I just feared the stigma attached to it. After all it was dark and mysterious, and most of all it was incurable.

So I listened and I learned. Not out of some sense of honor. No, I was twenty, and I knew little about honor. It was simply because I didn't want it. Nevertheless, I learned that it was not that easy to catch. I learned that it could not be transmitted through casual contact. I discovered that wearing my gloves and gown should be adequate protection. I feared less, but I still feared.

I had seen very few AIDS patients at the time, one, maybe two, probably more who didn't know yet. I'd heard more about them then I had actually treated them, but I knew they were out there. Selfishly, I didn't want them. Someone else could treat them. Someone else could deal with them.

But I got one.

We were called on this morning to a "Jack and the Box" fast food restaurant. It was out of our town and in the neighboring city of Lynwood, but since our paramedic units were on other runs, the mantle fell to us, the next closest unit.

I remember the morning vividly. It was overcast, foggy with a slight mist, and uncharacteristically cold for a Southern California morning. We raced through the mid morning traffic, dodging cars as they dodged us.

As we pulled up to the scene a Lynwood fire captain came to greet us. He wore a smirk on his chiseled face. "Make sure you guys glove up," he said, "she's got AIDS."

"What's wrong with her?" I asked.

"I don't know. Didn't talk to her."

I clutched my medical box and walked through the front door, only to be met by the restaurant owner. I could tell he was agitated. "You've got to take her out of my store," he hollered in a middle-eastern accent, "She cannot stay here."

I tried to ignore him. "Where is she?" I asked.

"There." He pointed to a table to my right. "She's got to go."

I glanced over and saw the firemen encircling the table where she sat, forming what, I presumed, was the five foot "protective ring". No one was talking to her. No one was helping her. One of them reminded me again in a sarcastic tone to "make sure I have my gloves on."

They cleared out as my partner and I approached. She sat alone at the booth. Head down.

"What's the problem Ma'am?" I asked as I sat down in the booth across from her.

She lifted her eyes slowly. "Aren't you afraid you're going to catch something from me?" she asked with a painfully sarcastic tone. She forced an uncomfortable smile.

"No Ma'am," I lied. "What seems to be the problem?"

She became slightly irritated. "I was cold, OK. Sorry to bother everyone." She put her head back down to the table.

I didn't know what to say. So I just looked at her for a few seconds. She was somewhere around thirty years old and couldn't have weighed ninety pounds. She had no teeth—I noticed that when she spoke. She had no jacket. She was dirty.

"Do you need to go to the hospital?" I asked routinely, hoping to get out of there.

"No," She replied.

"Do you have somewhere you can go?"

"No, my family has nothing to do with me and I got evicted."

"How'd you get AIDS?" I asked, not knowing why I asked. Maybe it was because she was not the 80's stereotype gay man.

She raised her arm to reveal track marks. She then pulled her other arm out from the table revealing a baggie clutched in her hand.

"What's that for?" I asked.

"It's all I have."

In the baggie was dried macaroni. Raw, uncooked, and dry. This was her breakfast. This was her life. I remember my heart skipping a beat when I saw the bag, for this was all she had with her. No water to boil it in. No sauce to pour over it. No warm garlic bread. Nothing.

Oh yea, and no teeth to eat it with.

But she tried.

Her eyes were so vacant. Her life had been scarred and taken away by addiction and disease. She was hurting. She needed a hand, a kind word, and a friend–even if only for a minute.

I wanted to reach out. I really did. I wanted to buy her something to eat; maybe then they would have let her stay. I wanted to take her home and give her a warm bed. I wanted to take my jacket off and give it to her. I wanted to help. I really did.

But what would the other guys think? And after all, I can't really get involved. That's taboo in our field. And if I buy her something to eat I won't have any money later. Of course, I need my jacket for work today. Someone else will help her.

Yea someone else.

So I went home.

Somewhere a short time later it hit me. It hit me hard. I remembered what I'd done that day. I'd walked away. Walked away when she needed me. I vowed to never walk away again. I have never forgotten her face.

I imagine that she went home too, home for good. I wonder if she knows I think about her all the time. I wonder if she knows I really did care about her. I wonder if she knew I cried for her. I wonder if she knows I have changed. I wonder if she knows I am glad that she's alright now.

I wonder if she knows I'm sorry.

~ TERROR AT MIDNIGHT ~

Only once in my career can I recall being absolutely petrified. I'd had dangerous situations before, and I have been scared, but not for my life. I've had to wrestle with many a patient and even been threatened in many ways by bystanders and family members. I had stood on scene in the LA projects with no where to run or hide, treating gunshot victims, when the crowd scattered and the police grabbed for their guns. But this night was "it", the one time I really felt scared for my life.

We had beat LA's squad 16 to the call. I have no idea how, I don't recall exactly, but we must have been in the area returning from a previous call. The call was in an area of LA just near Watts. It was not far from 16's station, but far from our station in Southgate. They didn't station us in the LA area because of the dangers involved. So we responded from the Southgate station. It always seemed that fire beat us to the scene on any call to our west. I guess squad 16 must have been out on something else when this call came in. Nevertheless, we were there first.

The call was for a cardiac arrest. There was no indication from dispatch of any danger. We arrived at the scene of a dark and dilapidated house-yet a house that was occupied by probable drug users for it had all the markings of a crack house. The sheriff would later confirm that this is exactly what it was. There was not a single light on anywhere.

We ran up to the front door with our gear and were met by an angry crowd of people. I couldn't tell you how many because all I could see was shadows and hear voices. They led us to a young lady about thirty, lying lifeless on the floor. She was in full cardiac arrest.

As we checked the pulse and readied the ambu-bag in pure darkness, one of the people in the house pushed me on my shoulder from behind to get my attention. "She dies; you die," he kept repeating to me, over and over again, undoubtedly threatening me. He was anxious and agitated, obviously high. Drugs and cardiac arrests can be a volatile mixture.

As my eyes adjusted I could see others in the room, pacing back and forth, some screaming at us to "DO SOMETHING!" The same man behind me, just over my shoulder, still repeating, "If she dies; you die."

At the time I believed him. Somehow in the darkness I could see the flash of a metal pistol in his waistband as he paced the floor behind me like one of those tigers at the zoo, eager for any reason to pounce. I believe he wanted me to see it. I know I didn't want to get shot, that's for sure. So my partner and I worked frantically. I remember telling the man, my voice cracking, "We are resuscitating her. She's gonna have to go to the hospital though." I knew a dead body when I saw one, but I had to play it out. I figured that if he was stupid enough to kill the caregiver, than he might just be stupid enough to believe that we were actually saving her. I wish we would have really been saving her, but I knew in all probability she was gone. I prayed for 16's and the sheriff to arrive. It seemed like an eternity for them to get there. "We're doing all we can," I tried to reassure the anxious man, hoping to buy more time.

16's finally got there, as did the sheriff. Lucky for me the threatening guy disappeared into the darkness after the Sheriff arrived. We eventually transported the patient over to Martin Luther King Hospital's emergency room. She didn't survive.

Thank Heaven's I did.

~ WITNESS TO A TRAGEDY ~

It was my partner's turn to be "patient man". That meant that all I had to do was drive—unless there was cleanup to do in the back of the ambulance. On this particular call there wasn't, so I put the gurney away and sat in the front of the ambulance, my door open, listening to the radio. Hey, I was young, and somehow I thought that playing the rock and roll loud would bring the girls around, especially for a "man in uniform". Unfortunately, my off duty life told me that this wasn't so, but I was willing to try anyway.

As I sat there outside the Saint Francis emergency room (Lynwood, California) listening to the radio, I heard the familiar sound of sirens coming up the street. One learns to recognize the different sirens and I knew that this wasn't one of our units. It could tell that it also wasn't a Lynwood fire truck so I hopped out of my seat to have a look. I always wanted to see who was rolling by-I guess you could say I am somewhat of an "ambulance chaser".

The ER's ambulance parking was situated just a few yards from the Century Boulevard/Imperial Boulevard intersection, so I had a perfect look as the siren got louder and neared the intersection. I could see it was a Los Angeles County Sheriff unit. He blazed up to the intersection and then suddenly skidded to a halt, right exactly in the middle of the intersection. The short, stocky Hispanic officer flung his door open and got out and stood behind it, his gun drawn and propped between the door and the car, aiming north. It happened so quickly, literally within seconds, but I heard the officer yell, "Drop the gun! Drop the gun!" I turned to look at where he was aiming and at that instant I heard two gunshots in quick succession. It was that fast. As my eyes focused around I saw the victim go down, right at

30

the edge of the adjacent crosswalk and on the lip of the curb. There was a gun lying nearby the fallen man.

The officer carefully ran over to the victim. I saw him kick the gun away and check on the victim, who was lying supine on the ground. Absolutely no one else was near them. Many people were now watching, but only the officer and the victim were on the curb. The quick thinking officer looked up and over at the ER. Of course the only one he saw was me, standing there half-frozen, watching. He stood up and waved for me to come over. I thought about running inside and getting Rich, but I didn't want to make the officer mad, so I ran around to grab our medical box and then figured that Rich would realize what was going on. Luckily though, just as I was getting ready to run over to the downed victim, my partner Rich came out of the ER. "Hey a guy just got shot!" I hollered to him. "We need the paramedics!" And then I ran over to the victim as he told dispatch over the radio to send the paramedic unit.

The victim lay there on the curb, not really moving, but he was alive. I saw two perfect holes in his belly, just below the navel. I told him to sit still and not to move. I put him on oxygen—which was all I could really do at that point. I checked his blood pressure and other vital signs. He struggled for breath, but his blood pressure was maintaining. He sweated profusely. About that time our Lynwood paramedic unit Arrived and I helped them at the scene and then they rushed him over to Martin Luther King Hospital. The patient would end up dying after many hours in surgery.

After they had left the scene I had the chance to look around. The sheriff's officer stood with some colleagues who were comforting him. Rich had his camera out taking some pictures–he did that often on scene. He was focusing on the gun that lay in the street, just off the curb. I saw that it was a revolver.

It turns out that the victim had been threatening people with this gun in the Hamburger place, just across the street from the hospital. That's why this officer had responded. Apparently, as the officer pulled up he had seen the victim crossing the crosswalk with the revolver in his hand. As he yelled, "Drop the gun!" the victim, the mentally retarded victim, turned around with the gun and was shot. It also happened that the victim lived just a few doors down from where he was shot, in a psychiatric facility for those who were mentally disabled.

I remember seeing the officer talking to his colleagues and crying. I didn't know officers cried. But he had good reason to. Not that he did anything wrong. But I am sure had he known all the facts he may not have fired. Matter of fact, I know he wouldn't of even drawn his gun.

The victim's gun? It was revolver...A revolver with no chamber. No chamber means no bullets. No bullets mean he couldn't have really hurt anyone.

Except himself.

~ LIFE 101 ~

For years I dealt with other people's problems. I was there for them in there deepest darkest trials, at times when they cried out in pain, when they lost a loved one, and even when they took their last breath. I was there.

It's quite possible EMS was a great escape for me. Dealing with other's problems meant I didn't have to deal with my own. That and EMS was self-gratifying. It's true we can get spit on, thrown up on, bled on. We can get cursed at, yelled at, and hit at. Yet somehow through it all the praise still comes. People look to you. They need you. They keep calling you.

But I did have problems of my own. Problems I couldn't find an answer to. Problems that kept me awake at night, that gave me ulcers at age sixteen, and that caused me to bury myself in this lifestyle that we call EMS.

I knew what to do when a stranger was bleeding to death. I could revive them when they stopped breathing. I could pull them from any position out of any car. I could save them. And even though I was trained to save untold lives, I couldn't save the one person who gave me life.

My own Mother.

I took a day off one afternoon. My mother had agreed to get help for her addiction to prescription drugs. Her life was a complete wreck. She couldn't have weighed 90 pounds. My little brothers and sisters were suffering incredibly at home, if it wasn't for my sisters Gina and Kathryn they would have suffered even worse. They took care of each other for the most part. Oh, she undoubtedly loved us–all eight of us (I was the oldest at 19 and Martin the youngest at 2), but prescription drugs became her great escape. I could tell you all the names. There was Valium, Codeine, Librium, Xanax. Those were her favorites. I marveled that the doctors kept giving them to her. Didn't they know? They had to have known—after all they were the doctors. But she paid and they gave and gave.

I should have been there at home more often I guess, especially for my little brothers and sisters, but I was a nineteen-year-old, confused, young man. I was trying to make my ends meet on $3.35 an hour. I was still practically in puberty.

I guess I was selfish too.

But that day I spent the last of the money I had to buy her a couple of new outfits. She was embarrassed to go into a rehab with ratty clothes, and she agreed to go if I would buy her some new clothes. Naturally I agreed. We needed to get her into something if she was to survive. I couldn't take it anymore. She had tried suicides, accidentally overdosed, and one night I came home to find her passed out on the toilet seat—I actually thought she was dead at first. It had to come to an end.

But we were poor and poor people are sometimes at the mercy of others. Mom didn't have health insurance. Dad had been out of work for a while, and even though he was working now (as an EMT for Southland Ambulance no less), there was no insurance and no money. We drove around Southern California looking for a rehab that would take her. We went to UC Irvine Medical Center and they told us that they didn't treat that kind of addiction. I remember the lady there telling us that if she was addicted to cocaine, heroin, or alcohol, it would be easy to get her in, but it was prescription drugs and there was nothing they could do. We went to a private rehab center, where they told us that they didn't take Medicaid, which would be our only chance for insurance. We drove all around to any place we thought could help her and they all told us the same thing—we need money or a new addiction. And we had neither to offer them.

All we saw was a brick wall.

And then it got worse from there.

Social services got involved. They had actually been out a few times to my parent's house before. A "friend" had called them reporting my parents for neglect. The last time they came they told my mother that they would be back to take the kids away. Mom had enough sense to not let that happen. So in the middle of the night she left with my Aunt, her only sister, and ran with the kids to Arizona. We three oldest stayed behind, as did my father, to work and go to school.

It seemed for awhile that things would get better. She found a house and it was clean. We'd drive up there on weekends and see her. The last time I spent time with her she was completely sober. She was so happy. It had been a long time since I saw her like that. We laughed, talked, and had a good time. She made a wonderful dinner, something she hadn't done in years. Things looked good.

Real good.

Then the phone call came.

I was at the station when she called. She had borrowed money from some neighbors she hardly knew in Arizona to fly to California. She had to see her "doctor". And once again, she paid and he gave. She left my little brother and little sisters in the care of my teenage sister Gina, who was only 14, and strangers. She needed to get back, but she had only taken a one way flight. I had no money and I had to work. I told her to get someone to help her get back. But they wouldn't help her since she was high as a kite. She had made a fool of herself again. Everyone else had had enough too. Her friends had long since abandoned her.

She was alone.

But she kept calling and calling the station, telling me that she had to get home. I remember arguing with her on the station's payphone. So finally I told my supervisor I had to go home. She always won. I had the choice to stay, but she would make the night miserable for everyone. If I took the phone off the hook she would call dispatch. So there was nothing else I could do. High, she made life miserable for everyone. So I had to go home to solve another problem. My Dad and I finally agreed that he would drive her back to Arizona with my car. He didn't have one at the time and had been living at one of the Southland Ambulance stations— though he wasn't supposed to be. I picked him up and as he drove me back home I remember yelling, "Why doesn't God just take her!" I couldn't take it anymore.

They left. I slept. About 1 am I heard a knock at the door. It shocked me at first and I noticed that my roommate Anthony didn't get up to answer the door. He could have slept through a hurricane. So I quickly ran downstairs to get it, not suspecting what I was about to hear. "Who is it?" I asked through the door.

"It's your Father," the voice on the other side replied.

I opened the door to see him standing there. He spoke first. "Your Mother's dead." He looked straight down. That's all he said.

"Come in," I said, swinging the door wide open. "What happened?" I asked, amazingly calm. Sadly, I was almost really relieved, for I knew that there was no other way she'd find peace.

He related to me the story. They'd pulled over and she'd somehow gotten into the traffic. It was night. A semi hit her and killed her. She died in a drugged stupor, but now she was free from her addiction.

And I would never see my Mother again.

And now I stood on the other side.

~ QUESTIONS ~

Michael and I were not even a mile away when the call came in. Mike was my partner at Southland Ambulance years before, and now we found ourselves working as partners again at Adams Ambulance Service in Los Angeles County. We were stationed in the city of Lakewood at the time. We had a much better time working the 24-hour shifts for Adams then we did working the 12-hour night shifts at Southland. We were good friends, we were both still young, and we both liked to have a good time.

But we wouldn't have a good time on this call.

Since we were so close to the call we beat the fire department there. In some ways we were excited to get there first. You think we would have learned our lesson through our prior experiences at Southland Ambulance, but we didn't. We still wanted to get there first. And the dispatch information only made the adrenaline flow faster.

It was a gunshot wound.

We pulled up to the house in the Lakewood neighborhood within minutes. One Los Angeles County Sheriff's unit was parked outside. We got out of our unit and ran into the house, clutching our little medic box and our oxygen tank. The sheriff met us as we went in the front door. Before we could ask any questions he told us, "I think she's gone, but you'd better have a look." He directed us to a tiny little back room off of the kitchen. The room was the size of a large closet. On the floor next to the bed lay the body of an 18-year-old girl. In her hand was a large revolver. The smell of gunpowder was unmistakable.

It was Mike's turn to confirm what we already knew, but he didn't move. He was supposed to enter the small room and check the patients pulse. Both of us stood there looking into the room and neither of us was moving. A dark pall hung in the air.

"It's your turn, bro," I told Mike, but he just stood there. I didn't want to do it and I know he didn't want to do it, so I reminded him again, just in case he forgot whose turn it was. "It's your turn, Mike."

"I'm not going in there. She's dead," he replied.

"I know, but we have to check."

But he didn't move. Somehow he got me to do the dirty work again. He always did that to me. But I knew we had to check her out, even though death was obvious.

So I gingerly entered the room. The smell of gunpowder and the whole atmosphere freaked me out. She lay there, gun still in hand, bullets spilled on the floor next to her. She had shot herself in the head. Her eyes were still open. Her body was warm. I was too freaked out to reach up to her neck and check her carotid pulse, so I reached for arm. There was no pulse. I wish there would have been, but there wasn't. So I backed out of the room.

Mike was already ahead of me; back in the front room headed toward the door where we had came in. But someone had stopped him on his way out. As I came toward the room I could hear yelling from the living room.

It was the girl's father. He had cornered Mike.

I entered the front room and was instantly approached by the father. He had somehow hoped that we could do something, anything. He was looking to us to help his daughter. He doesn't know how bad I wanted to be able to.

He hollered in my face, "you have to do something for my baby!"

I tried to stay calm. I know he was hurting. "Sir, there isn't anything we can do."

He shoved a piece of paper, the girl's report card, in both Mike's face and mine. "See this?" he yelled, "See this. She had straight A's. Why would she do this?"

All we could do is shrug our shoulders. At that moment we were not lifesavers, or heroes, or anything special. We were just people. Two people who couldn't do anything at all to help another's pain.

But how we wanted to.

He continued to yell and scream. He wanted her to be healed, to get up and to come out to him. But she never would again.

At that moment I didn't want to be the first one there anymore

~ A Deeper Love ~

A middle-aged gentleman met us at the door. He wore a concerned look on his face, but not one that was frantic or overly panicked. At the time this struck me as odd, for the dispatch information told us that we had a cardiac arrest inside the house. Normally the scene is one of chaos and confusion in these situations.

I relaxed a little, thinking that dispatch must have been given some wrong information.

He swung the screen door open wide as we approached with our equipment. "She's in the back room," he said, "I think she died."

"Why do you say she died?" I asked him as I worked my way through the hall and toward the back room.

"She's been sick for awhile." He stopped and pointed to the room. "She's in there. On the bed."

I looked into the room. Centered in the middle of the room was a lone hospital bed upon which our patient lay. Thin and gaunt, her hair all gone except for a little wisps that lay atop her head. She lay still. Years of training told me, even before I reached her side, that this didn't look right. I watched her chest as I approached the bed. But I saw nothing. The normal up and down movement that gives us life had ceased sometime before we arrived. I checked her pulse.

Nothing.

The man who let us in stood at the doorway. Our eyes looked into each other's. "Is there anything you can do?" he asked, hoping. Yet somehow I knew that he already knew the answer.

"Can you tell me what happened?" I asked professionally as I hooked up the EKG to her chest.

"She's had cancer. She was having some trouble breathing earlier, but I didn't know this was going to happen." He looked down at the floor.

I looked up at my partner Eric and shook my head slightly. This was all the signal that he needed to call dispatch and tell them that our patient was deceased. Now came the part that I consider the hardest aspect of my duties as a paramedic. I had to tell him that his beloved wife had passed on.

"Sir," I said, "I'm so sorry. She's passed away."

He looked up at me calmly. "I know. It's been expected, but it still hurts so much."

"I'm sorry," I said again.

He walked over to the bed and picked her head up in his arms, gently kissing her forehead. "I love you," he said, "It's alright now. No more pain." He kissed her again.

I sat down in a corner of the room in the only chair, and watched. He explained to me that he had just sent the nurse away, that she had been working hard and needed a break. He didn't expect this to happen though. He told me that he'd brought her home to be with him. He couldn't have her far from him in some nursing home and that he needed to be by her side. As he tenderly straightened her gown he related to me that he'd lost his job and that their finances had greatly suffered since her illness, but that this is what love was all about. I could tell that he wasn't complaining, just simply making a statement.

I marveled as he held her again, kissing her forehead one last time. It was a sad time yet somehow happy. He loved her. It shone in his eyes. There was no denying it. The physical attractiveness that she once held had been ravaged by cancer, only to be replaced by a deeper and truer love that even in death did not part.

I watched with tears in my eyes, realizing that he may never know the lesson he was teaching. A lesson about love, about sacrifice, about giving, about service. Life lessons that are beyond any classroom.

He lay her head gently to the pillow. "I love you," he said again, tears in his eyes.

And somehow I believe she heard him.

~ House Calls ~

Bryon and I had barely enough time to make sure our equipment was on the unit when the call came in. We were to respond to the Prattville area, one of the areas at the far Western edge of our response area, to a doctors office in that little town. It was still early and my first thought was that someone had driven up to the office needing help. Indeed, dispatch told us that we had a "chest pain".

Often times, someone needing help in the outlying areas would drive up to a clinic or doctor's office, or even a fire station to get or to call for help. I figured that this had to be another one of those situations.

But stupid me, I should have known that when it comes to medicine one should never jump to conclusions.

We pulled into the office parking lot and were directed by one of the assistants. She showed us where to park and which door to enter into. I thought she would lead us to some patient under the Doctor's care, but upon entering his small office we soon discovered that nobody had pulled up to get help that early morning. Not this time, for it wasn't some rural patient we were called out there for and it wasn't some passing traveler—it was the Doctor we were there for.

He sat in a chair in one of his rooms. I tried to be very respectful, asking, "What's wrong, Doctor?" He looked pale and uncomfortable. He didn't say much, just telling me that his, "Chest hurt." He continued to fidget in the chair. Experience told me that something just wasn't right with him. He was way too quiet for a doctor. I leaned down and felt his pulse, what I could feel of it, and it was extremely faint and distant. Blood pressure revealed a low one, in the 70's systolic. The Doctor told me that he felt an intense pain and a tearing sensation. I feared the worst–an aneurysm.

I looked at the Doctor and told him of my concern asking him if "there was anything special he wanted me to do?" I then told him "Otherwise I am just going to treat you according to protocol." He didn't say anything; he just looked up and shook his head. At that Bryon and I quickly started a large bore IV of normal saline. I knew time was critical, but with his pressure so low I was deeply concerned about moving him too quickly and hurting him worse. He didn't argue or complain. I felt so bad for him because it was obvious that he needed help. We worked as fast as we could. I pumped some fluid into him just to maintain his pressure as we moved him. I explained my protocol to him with every move and treatment.

A couple of times Bryon asked me if we should give him some morphine for the pain. I ignored him at first thinking that he just didn't understand the situation, but as he continued to ask I finally told him firmly, "We aren't giving him morphine with his pressure this low!" I was concerned about giving it to him and dropping the pressure even further, which could possibly kill him.

We loaded him quickly and got underway. I knew that without surgery this good doctor would not survive. He obviously knew it long before I did. Enroute to Tulsa Regional Hospital he stayed fairly stable and conscious, but his pain never did subside. We dropped him off at the osteopathic hospital where he was among colleagues and friends, for the Doctor himself was a D.O.

They soon discovered that he had a descending aortic aneurysm. He was in surgery within a couple of hours and thankfully he survived.

Now I have often heard that healthcare workers make the worst patients, with doctors heading the top of the list. I don't think that this statement is necessarily true, and on this morning good old Dr Russell was the model patient. I am grateful we were able to help him. I met his son some time later and he told me that he had retired after that, but thank goodness retirement doesn't mean death.

~ MESSAGE IN A BOTTLE ~

The page came across our pagers as someone who may have injured his penis. Now we did not get injuries involving the genitalia very often, but when they did happen it usually meant something very bizarre was going on. This would be no exception.

As we climbed the stairs to the victim's apartment a group of teenagers met us before we got to the door. "What happened we asked?" We were a three man crew that day, myself, my partner, and Mike, a "returnee" who was now orientating with me. Mike had worked at the service before, quit, and now he'd come back. They still required him to go back through the orientation process, and since I was a training officer they put him with me.

"My Grandpa's hurt himself," one of them said.

We walked past the teenagers and into the run-down apartment. Empty beer cans and bottles filled the kitchen and the smoke filled living room. And there, in the living room, on the couch, sat our patient, smoking a cigarette.

"What's wrong?" Mike asked him.

The old man sat there naked, still smoking. He pointed between his legs. "My thing's broke." He told us, as if we should know already. He spread his legs to reveal the largest, most purplest, most swollen, object between anyone's legs I had ever seen. There were cuts and blood along the sides of it.

"What happened?" We asked, probably in unison.

He was in no real mood to talk. I don't think I would be either. "I put it in a coke bottle," he said curtly, "And it got stuck."

No kidding. Further inspection revealed that he made numerous attempts to get the bottle off. He actually got the bottle off, but the hard

45

glass ring stayed at the base of the penis. He couldn't get that off. I guess he forgot that it would get bigger. He was in his sixties, but he told us he was high on crank. He had to be, in my opinion, to put his penis in a bottle. The bathroom sink was bloody and filled with glass. He'd used pliers, hammers, scissors, you name to try and get the bottleneck off. It would finally come off with a ring cutter at the ER.

That was one of the hardest radio reports I ever gave. Believe me, there are times you want to, but you just can't laugh. How do you tell the ER that you have a man who put his penis in a coke bottle and now has the glass ring stuck on his penis? Well, You tell the ER that you have a man who stuck his penis in a coke bottle and now has the glass ring stuck on his penis.

Then you laugh later.

~ HAPPY BIRTHDAY ~

I lay in the back of the ambulance taking a little "nap". We were posted at our Sand Springs post, which was the furthest west for our response area. We ran many calls in the rural areas out there, some of them requiring very long response times. Of course, it helps if people out in the real rural areas give us directions, which they sometimes do, but it sure complicates things when they are not sober. Like on this night.

As I lay in the back trying to kill some time–we only had about an hour until our shift would be over–I heard dispatch come over the radio...stand by for a possible gunshot, they told us. Thad, my partner that night, answered them with the customary "10-4."

I sat up and brushed the sleepies from my eyes. Poking my head through the porthole window, I asked Thad, "What's up?"

"They said they had a possible gunshot for us," he told me, "But that's all they said."

After a few minutes I jumped front into my seat. Still no word had come from dispatch so I asked them over the radio, "Do you have something for us?"

Dispatch replied that they had a difficult caller on the radio and were having a very difficult time getting information. A few seconds later they came back on and told us to "start west on the Keystone." The "Keystone" was the name for highway 64.

We pulled out of the Quick Trip parking lot and raced down the highway into the dark cold night–it was the dead of winter. Dispatch came back on and told us that someone will meet us at the convenience store along the highway. They didn't know the name of it, but a car would meet us there and take us to the scene.

About that time, I told Thad that the only convenience store that I knew of was at the next exit, which we were getting ready to pass. He swerved the ambulance over to the side and barely made the exit. As soon as we pulled off, there was the car. It was a dark Monte Carlo type car with the windows tinted. An arm waved into the darkness from the half rolled down driver's window, beckoning for us to follow. We wanted to pull up next to it to ask some questions, but the car took off north at a high rate of speed. As we both raced down the highway we struggled to keep up with the swerving, nearly out-of-control car. And unfortunately, we could see no one inside because of the tint and the outside darkness. We didn't know if we were dealing with one person or two or three–we had no idea how many. To make matters worse, dispatch told us that Osage County Sheriff gave them a one-hour ETA. They also told us that Sand Springs Police were not responding as it was out of their area.

So what do we do? We could go in and take a chance following this crazy dark car in front of us, or we could turn around and wait for PD–and then take a chance on the car coming back and doing who knows what to us.

We followed the car.

It seems that we went north for mile after mile. It is a very rural area, with no streetlights and rarely street signs. The mysterious car in front of us swerved and crossed the line a number of times. I was wondering how soon we'd be working a car wreck. Then finally, the car turned down another dark road, headed due east. We followed as fast as we could as the car drove down this dark, dirt, road. After about a half a mile it suddenly stopped and pulled to the edge of some long driveway. We thought that we were finally here, but the car backed up and then started coming back toward us. I thought that my life was over at this point. As it neared the driver's side Thad rolled down the window and waved for the car to stop.

The car stopped.

Finally, we could see the driver. It was a middle-aged woman who slurred her words as she spoke. "I made a wrong turn," she said. We started to ask her what was going on, but she rolled up her window and took off again, back to the road were we had originally been on. She headed north. A short ways up she turned back east again and barreled down another dirt road. Through the dust I saw her pull into another long driveway. We followed form a short distance back, driving slowly just in case of a contingency. I saw her pull up next to a pitch-black house, except for one little light in the front room. The skies were dark outside as clouds concealed the moon and stars.

She jumped out of her car and ran into the house, through a sliding glass door to where the light was. We parked a good distance back–leaving plenty of room to run. I opened my door and stood behind it. I remember thinking that I could make out of the driveway in seconds and to cover if I needed to. Somehow we always think we can outrun a bullet. We waited for the lady to come back out. Finally she stepped out frantically waving her arm, yelling, with slurred speech again, "Get in here!"

I yelled to her, "Lady, what's going on?" without leaving my spot behind the door.

"He's shot." She told me, "Get in here."

"Who shot him?"

"He shot himself," she replied.

"Where's the gun?" I yelled.

"We have it. Get in here."

Thad and I grabbed the gear and headed toward the house. I was really frightened with my heart beating in my chest. We should have been frightened. I knew that there would be no police officer arriving in a few minutes and I couldn't afford body armor-some might say I can't not afford it, but when it comes down to feeding your family or buying a bullet proof vest, I chose to feed my family. There wasn't even the luxury of extra bodies to help, since no firefighters had shown up.

We slowly approached the door. Peeking in carefully I could see two ladies, each of them yelling for us to hurry. A man was on the floor at the far end of the room, half-kneeling on the carpet, blood pouring from his face.

And disgustingly, two small dogs stood there licking at the puddles of blood pooling on the floor. A pistol sat on the cabinet, out of the patient's reach.

We ran to the patient's side. I told Thad to call for a helicopter immediately and to get someone to set up a landing zone. Thank heavens that while we were following the car I had scouted a landing zone at the main road and this road we had turned down. That would be where we needed to sit the chopper down at. Dispatch told us that Sand Springs fire department was on the way. We were clearly out of their district, but they knew we needed help. There were only two of them on the rescue squad, but I was never so glad to see them come through the door.

"What do you got?" one of them asked me.

"He's shot himself," I told them. "We are going to need an L.Z. The bird's on the way." I looked at the both of them and told them, "I saw a good spot back there at the road," like I was some kind of genius–that was really the only spot. I am confident they would have found it anyway.

They raced out of the door. The next time we would see them would be at the landing zone. I turned to the patient, "How are you breathing?" I asked. He said he was doing "alright". Blood continued to drain from his nose and mouth and on to the carpet. I could see a bulge near his right eye. His vital signs were stable, but given the nature of his injury I knew that he could go downhill at any time. After all, there was a bullet somewhere in his cranium. There was no exit wound.

Thad and I hurried and packaged the patient for transport. Time was essential here. The only thing that was going to help him was surgery. We loaded him onto gurney, sitting him up so the blood could drain out of his mouth and nose. There is no way for us to stop bleeding of that kind. As we bounced down the road toward the landing zone I started an IV-just in case things did go downhill. I prayed that Sand Springs fire had done their job in landing the helicopter.

As we pulled up to the landing zone I saw that the two guys from the fire department had done their job perfectly. The landing zone was lit up in some farmer's field, exactly where I had scouted it out. The helicopter was just touching down as we arrived. We drove our ambulance over the grass and parked close to the landing zone. The helicopter crew met us at the unit and we transferred the patient to the helicopter crew.

Then we rested.

Our supervisor had driven out there to see what had happened. A Sand Springs police officer did finally show up, but just to see what was going on. I never saw an Osage County sheriff–at least I didn't notice one. For a moment all the lights of the emergency vehicles lighted the whole scene up against the clouds. Oddly, no neighbors came outside to investigate the commotion. I figure that that would be a good place for a UFO to land if they didn't want to be detected. One by one though the other vehicles pulled away, leaving Thad and I standing there, cleaning up the unit.

And then it started to snow.

I remember sitting there on the back of the unit with Thad. We were sweating and tired, but the scene was almost surreal. We just sat there for a moment talking and resting and debriefing. The glow of our lights, combined with the falling snow and the still flowing adrenaline, made it a picture worth a thousand words. And above all we had helped save a life.

Yet as we sat there I remembered some words one of the ladies told us as we worked on the patient in the house. She said that the patient was upset because he couldn't be with his son that day so he shot himself in the head. That's why he did it.

It was his son's birthday.

Hum…I just buy mine a present.

~ ALMOST HOME ~

The driver was reportedly swatting at a wasp when she swerved across the centerline and struck the motorcyclist. Only less than mile from his home, the poor motorcyclist was struck by the mini-van and thrown into the bushes on the side of the road.

That's when we got called.

By the time we had arrived at the scene the Tulsa Fire Department first responders were already on scene trying to assess the situation. My partner Jim and our paramedic orientee Cameron jumped out of the front of the unit and ran to the scene. Cameron and I had already decided that if it was bad we wouldn't hesitate to call the helicopter, since it was rush hour at the time and we didn't want to delay transport of the patient while fighting traffic.

It took about two seconds to realize it was bad.

I jumped out of the back and pulled the gurney out. By that time Cameron had already called the helicopter. I calmly walked over near the scene to check things out and saw that they had a critically ill patient, thought he was still conscious. A firefighter stood nearby me at the edge of the road. I turned to him and told him, "We're going to have to get him off of that tree limb." The fireman looked at me funny and walked away. From a distance I looked again at the scene that was slightly on an incline below us. At first I could have swore that the patient's leg was impaled on a tree limb, but a second glance told me that it wasn't a tree limb I was seeing, it was the patients bone sticking out. He'd amputated his leg.

I walked down to the scene to find three men in addition to my partner working on the patient. The leg was still attached by only a skin flap, but the bleeding was very minimal. Apparently, before I had arrived, the fire captain had asked Cameron if he wanted a tourniquet on the patient's leg. Since bleeding was so slight, he said no. It is important to keep blood flow going to the limb just in case it can be reattached. A tourniquet may not have kept that blood flow going. Cameron knew that, as he was one of the sharpest medics I ever orientated.

When I climbed down to the scene, the captain must have recognized me as the "senior" medic and asked me again if I wanted a tourniquet. I told him know also, qualifying it with; "we need to keep the blood flowing."

So we worked feverishly trying to package the patient for transport. He wasn't complaining much, but he seemed a little lethargic to us on scene. The most important thing was to keep him alive and then get him somewhere where they could reattach the leg. We started an IV while waiting for the chopper to set down in a nearby field and gave him a little fluid. As Cameron continued to assess the patient I looked down at the patient's leg and couldn't believe what I saw.

A tourniquet.

It was a dirty piece of tape that was into the tissue of the leg where the injury had occurred. It wasn't really tight enough to help anyway, but it was cutting into his already damaged flesh.

I lost my cool for a moment. "Who the hell put this tourniquet on him? I thought we said no tourniquet!" I hollered. Jim stood nearby with his scissors and I hollered to him as the Lifelight medics got out of the helicopter and came toward us, "Cut that thing off." He did and the patient's pain seemed to lessen slightly.

We turned the patient over to the helicopter crew and they took the patient to Saint Francis Hospital. Unfortunately they were unable to save his leg. Fortunately, he survived.

After the chopper had lifted off I turned to the fire captain and asked very politely, "Why did you guys put that tourniquet on after I said no?"

He looked up at me, "I'm sorry, but the doctor said to do it."

"What doctor?" I asked.

He handed me the card that the doctor had given him and pointed to a guy across the street getting into his car. He had on a dark navy blue jacket. One that looked exactly like the one the Tulsa firefighters wear. We thought he was another fireman. He never identified himself to us. Undoubtedly I would have respected his wishes had I known. I may not have agreed with him, but I would have respected him. He had that right as a doctor. But he never said a word to any of us medics at the scene.

Maybe that was best of all. His card said his specialty was adolescent medicine.

And our patient was an adult.

~ CHANGES ~

She changed my career.

She changed my life.

I think she was the reason I didn't want to do this anymore.

I must admit that I never thought that it could happen to me—this thing that we call burnout. After all, I loved my job. And I loved being a paramedic. I truly enjoyed serving others. And I absolutely refused that it was happening to me.

Not me. No way.

This was all I had known since high school. I'd never really done anything else, and at this point in my career I'm not so sure I can remember wanting to do something else. This job, this career, this entity that we call EMS, became my life.

She would change all of that in less than a half-hour.

It was a clear day. A day that just made one feel good inside. That made one feel like sucking in the warmth of the sun under some giant oak tree, while letting the wind whisper a soothing song through the leaves and over the green grass. Oh, how I could sleep peacefully under that tree.

But that would have to wait, for I had work to do. Important work. Work that saved lives and gave hope. Work that made me feel like I had a purpose, that I was important. Thus duty called. Literally.

We responded to a local apartment complex close to our location.—trouble unknown. We turned on our lights and sirens and headed that way, only to have our call upgraded to a high priority "auto versus pedestrian" accident. The very nature of these calls made them a high priority, and usually they turned out fine, so I remained fairly unconcerned. I even commented to my partner, telling her that I run calls like these in apartment complexes often and they usually amounted to nothing more than someone wanting to sue someone else.

Dispatch told us that we had an adult male.

We pulled into the parking lot and looked around. A man about 30 ran out of the office, screaming and waving his arms. We pulled up next to him and got out. The man continued to scream, telling me, "Hurry up, I think she's slipping. We're gonna lose her!"

Uh uh. Bystanders always panic.

I got out briskly, but not too overly quick and grabbed my Thomas Pack from the back. The man stood there, pleading for me to hurry.

Like I said, bystanders always panic.

I caught a glimpse of his eyes as he hollered at me. The eyes tell a lot to a paramedic, and I could see more than just panic in those eyes. I could see fear. My heart started to pound faster. Adrenaline. Hum, after all these years it still flowed. I ran up the steps to the office wondering what we had.

I expected a 30-year-old man.

I saw a 5-year-old girl. Blonde with blue eyes.

She was taking her last breath.

Something inside me was dying too.

But I knew what to do. I tried to intubate, but her teeth were clinched. I yelled for my partner to grab a c-collar and backboard, but she was already standing next to me with them in her hands. I hyperventilated the little girl with the BVM.

"Come on Honey," I said, "come on."

Tulsa Fire took over ventilations as I helped ready the patient for transport. We were less than a mile from Saint Francis Hospital, a trauma center and pediatric facility, and in my professional opinion, one of the nation's best.

We Loaded and drove. The Scene time was less than 5 minutes.

The fireman ventilated and I tried an I.V. while my partner drove. No go, her veins had collapsed. "Don't do this to me little girl," I thought selfishly, "I can't take it."

The monitor flashed PEA to asystole. Asystole. I know the stats—traumas don't survive asystole.

I started chest compressions.

I don't know why, but I turned to the fireman and told him over the sirens, "I can't do this anymore. This is it."

He didn't quite understand.

She was on the trauma bed for barely a minute before they pronounced her. The car had crushed her chest and there was no way to save her. I know that that same car crushed more than one chest.

We couldn't locate her parents. She was being babysat by her 16-year-old aunt who accidentally ran her over as she pulled the car away. It was a total accident. But the parents weren't there. I wanted to hold her and tell her that it was all right to go. That she was loved. That she was needed. I cried for her parents. I cried for me. I just cried.

I couldn't work any more that day, so I asked to go home. They brought me to the main office for Critical Incident Stress Debriefing. But I didn't want CISD that day. I wanted to go home. I needed to go home. I had a support group there.

So I went home, where I had something to do. Something very important.

I needed to hug my daughter.

My five year-old daughter.

My blonde haired, blue eyed daughter.

I told her that I loved her. That I needed her.

~ CLOSURE ~

EMS is full of irony. It also makes one realize how small the world can be.

For me it became even smaller one evening.

I must mention that I struggled with that call involving that little girl for a long time. I still struggle with it. I can't explain exactly why. She wasn't the first child I'd ever seen die nor would she be the last. Of course it's never easy, but I could always carry on. This time was different though. Now, whenever a pediatric call came in I panicked inside. I didn't want to take it; I wanted to run away from it. I caught myself crying at times while driving home. I was anxious and nervous with my own children. I guess we call this post traumatic stress disorder, but I kept my feelings to myself. I had a strong faith and felt as if I would eventually be all right. I was, but I needed some help along the way.

One evening as I got off shift our supervisor Jim asked if he could speak to me. Of course I said yes—you don't say no to your supervisor. Jim is a very caring man and well respected, possessing a real knack for "counseling." Jim told me that a few nights prior while out driving around he'd been approached by a lady who said that she needed to speak to me about her little girl who died. I got a lump in my throat. I knew who it was and what she wanted. He said that she said she'd been trying to contact me, but never heard from me. Indeed, I had gotten a few messages to call her, but I just couldn't. The pain from that run was too deep for me. I asked Jim if he'd call her for me, as this was something I couldn't do yet. I explained, briefly, the run and how difficult it was for me emotionally. I told him that I don't believe she suffered at all and that I did the best I could for her. He agreed to talk to her.

A month or so passed by and I asked Jim if he'd ever gotten the chance to talk to her. Unfortunately, he hadn't been able to. I still couldn't, so I went about my business. I believe she still had tried to contact me through administration, but I didn't get the messages.

Nearly a year after the incident I was still struggling inside. I guess professional help may have been beneficial, but I still relied on my family and faith to help me through this, even though I kept my feelings private. I know God is always mindful of His children and finds a way to help us whether we realize it or not.

I needed His help now.

I still had this profound anxiety every time a pediatric call came in. It was almost to the point where I was afraid that care would be compromised by my anxiousness. Somehow I managed to hide it from my partners. Lucky for me I had a wonderful partner in Mary. She was naturally bubbly and upbeat, and without knowing it she helped me through this. She was also my partner on this new night.

The call came in as an overdose. It was a 3 year-old boy who had taken some medication. We didn't know the status of the child, just that he'd taken some kind of prescription medication. My heartbeat jumped up and I became instantly anxious. I prayed inside as we drove, "Let everything be ok, let everything be ok.

We had quite a distance to travel to get to the call and since the patient lived a great distance south of our response area, the mother had driven closer, to a pay phone, to call 911. She had the child with her.

I recall the night was beautifully clear and mild.

Mary and I pulled up to the closed convenience store where the caller had said she would meet us. There, standing next to a parked car, was a lady in her late twenties to early thirties, a young teenage girl, and the patient, a little boy. The mother had her arms around the child as he sat on the hood of the car.

I approached the mother and began asking the usual questions that any paramedic would ask. I saw that the boy was very alert, not crying, and calm. Mother appeared very calm too. I relaxed a little.

As I began to ask my usual repertoire of questions the mother leaned forward and started yelling, "You're Jamie Bingham! You're Jamie Bingham!" I must admit I was caught off guard at first, but strangely, I quickly realized who she was. I do not know to this day how I knew what I knew, but I knew who she was. I'd never met her. I'd never seen her. But I knew.

It was her.

She asked me if I remembered her daughter.

I told her I'd never forgotten.

I asked Mary to take the boy and check him out. I pulled the mother aside and told her I'd like to talk to her. I hollered to Mary that we may be here for awhile. I didn't care if I lost my job that night. I would be there with her as long as she, the mother, needed me to be.

So we talked. Under the stars on a beautiful night we talked. She needed to know what happened. I needed to tell her.

I let her know that her daughter was never conscious and that she appeared to die peacefully. Not much of a consolation I know, but her mom needed to know. I assured her that myself and everyone else did all that we could. I told her of my struggles, letting her know that I realized it didn't compare to her loss and her pain.

And so we talked, we hugged, we cried. I don't know how long we were actually there, but it didn't matter. Her son was going to be fine. He'd only taken one pill and medical control assured us he'd be fine.

Yet she found closure and I found peace. That was what I needed. Someone knew exactly what it was that I needed.

Her son? He'd taken a pill the doctor had given to the mother to help her cope with her daughter's death. The same daughter I ran on. How's that for irony.

Oh yea, the teenage girl at scene? The aunt. The one who ran the little girl over. What a glorious attitude of forgiveness and understanding from the mom. She had forgiven. And now she knew exactly what had happened.

I looked up into the beautiful night sky. I believe that one of those million stars was her daughter looking down upon us that night.

Now I could move on.

THE AGREEMENT

The patient and I had an unspoken mutual agreement.

He wanted me to save him; I wanted to give him one more chance at life.

That was how it was supposed to work.

But it never works the way we want it to.

He had come into the Bank of Oklahoma building this morning to transact some routine business. He told me that he had felt fine earlier in the morning and didn't suspect any problems. But things would change shortly after entering the bank building. Ominous things neither that he nor I had any control over.

He wasn't without health issues. Sometime before his doctors had implanted in his chest an internal defibrillator to control an out of step heartbeat. He told me it hadn't really gone off before and it surprised him this morning when it went off after he entered the bank. Indeed, upon our entering the bank I could hear him moaning as it went off. Sadly, he could feel his heart began to race and he knew that within seconds the device in his chest would literally "shock" his heart. He told me this as I first approached him, warning me, "It's gonna do it again!" I jumped back, mainly on impulse, because I knew that it couldn't really shock me.

He started breathing heavy and then his body jerked up on the bench. His eyes rolled for a second and then he looked at me. "Help me," he pleaded.

He also sat all alone on a bench in a dark corner. No one had offered his or her assistance. Cynically, I wonder if the American way is "money first; people second." They did call 911 for him, which was at least helpful. I started asking him some general questions. "What is your history?" Do you have any pain?"

My partner Chuck and the Tulsa firemen put him on some oxygen and hooked up the cardiac monitor. He warned us again that his heart was racing and that he was going to be shocked. We all stepped back on impulse again and watched as his body jerked and heaved off the bench. "Can you do something for me?" he asked again.

I felt calm, self-assured, arrogant even. I had recently dealt with patients just like him and *I knew* that I could fix his problem. Just a short while before I had ran one the Tulsa fireman's father who had the same problem. I gave the fireman's father just one dose of Lidocaine, a drug used to control rapid and abnormal heartbeats, and was able to stop his internal defibrillator from shocking him. I just knew that this patient would be no different, after all he was only in his fifties and looked fairly healthy otherwise. I told him "Don't worry, you just need some Lidocaine."

Meanwhile his defibrillator shocked him again. He was also getting paler. "Don't let me die." He asked me, looking straight into my eyes. I know he wanted to live.

I know that I wanted to save him. "Not on my shift," I reassured him, trying to ease his fears. I just knew that he would make it.

We started the IV line and pushed the Lidocaine directly into his bloodstream. His defibrillator shocked him again anyway. Sometimes it takes a minute or two to work. He was getting weaker and paler. His body jerked again.

It wasn't working.

That's alright I thought, he just needs a second dose. I pushed the second dose into his veins again.

It still wasn't working. His defibrillator shocked him again. His eyes began to roll back in his head. "I'm gonna go out," he told me, "It's getting dark."

Remember, not on my shift. We laid him to the floor to help his blood pressure, which was now falling. His eyes still rolled back and his defibrillator still shocked him again. "Hang on, buddy," I told him, after all, it is my *job* to save people. I was determined that he would go home again.

Chuck quickly readied the Bretylium for me, the second drug to use if the first didn't work. Chuck was amazing; he was always one step ahead of the game. But suddenly, while we tried to move the patient to the gurney, a fireman tripped on the IV line and pulled it out. Chuck was on it, "Don't worry," he said, "I got it taken care off." With that he put the line back in place and the Bretylium was on board. But the patient's heart was still racing. I shocked him now with out defibrillator. Maybe he just needed a higher energy level I thought, and ours could be turned up high.

But it didn't work.

And the patient was unconscious.

We loaded him in the ambulance and raced to the hospital. I tried everything possible that I could do enroute to the emergency room. Everything. I kept telling him over the sirens to "just hang on," just in case he could hear me.

But he couldn't hang on.

And he was pronounced dead at the ER.

So I lied to him. He died on my shift after all.

And I broke our agreement.

~ All in the Family ~

Chris and I got the call in the late afternoon. At first I really couldn't believe what I had heard on the radio, a "shooting at an elementary school", but that is exactly what it was. On first impulse I naturally feared the worst. With all the sicko's and mentally deranged people in the world I thought that someone had opened fire on the children at the school. I prayed that it wasn't so, that all the children would be safe, but initially I just wasn't sure.

Dispatch told us that PD was already on the scene and that it was safe to enter. We still didn't know what we had and many thoughts ran through my mind as we approached the school.

As we rounded the corner to the schools parking lot I saw one lone police car at the scene. A crowd had also gathered along the edge of the tape. The female officer was out, already taping off the scene with the yellow tape–tape that tells you in an instant that something wasn't good. In the middle of the tape I caught a glimpse of a heap of clothing on the concrete. It wasn't moving.

I grabbed the cardiac monitor and ran up to the scene. The officer calmly told me, "He's already dead." I leaned down and looked at the patient below me. He lay there not moving. A trickle of blood oozed from a single gunshot wound to the chest. Per protocol and to cover my own rearend I hooked the patient up to the monitor and confirmed the obvious. He had been killed by that single gunshot wound to the chest.

Now I asked myself, "Why?"

About five feet from the body an elderly man sat in his pickup, the door wide open. He sat there calmly; just watching the events unfold. As I fiddled with my equipment the female officer came over and began talking to the man in the pickup. I overheard their conversation as the man related to the officer how he had been forced to shoot the other man when the now deceased man came at him with a pocketknife. Indeed, a small pocketknife lay on the ground next to the body.

Why did the man with the knife attack the man in the pickup, only to be shot in the process? Because they were arguing in the parking lot as they waited to pickup their grandson. I said *their* grandson. They were both grandfathers to the same boy. And each wanted to pick the grandson up. So they argued.

And the gun won. Sort of.

Neither got to pick up the grandson.

So no one won.

~ ONE OF OUR OWN ~

My partner Art and I, along with our colleagues working that morning, raced all over the city of Tulsa responding to emergencies on the rains slicked roads. Somehow we had freed ourselves up and we're headed up the Broken Arrow expressway when I heard my former partner Mary holler over the radio, "I'm gonna need a second unit!" There was apparently more to her conversation that neither Art nor I caught, but we did hear that she needed a second unit. As busy at it was that morning we knew that we would be heading that way.

Within seconds dispatch asked us our location. While we weren't necessarily close to their location on the 244, we were sent that direction, as we were one of the few units available. We jumped off the highway at the 15th street exit and raced up Lewis Avenue toward the 244. We caught the 244 at Lewis and headed toward Memorial Avenue, where the accident was reported to be. As we approached Memorial we realized that we could catch it best by crossing over the highway and opposing traffic. Since the accident had blocked the traffic coming our way we felt safe enough going the opposite direction on the highway.

As we approached the scene I noticed Mary and Jerry's unit off the side of the road. I asked Art, "Why did they park like that?" As we pulled a little bit more forward Art hollered, "Look!"

I glanced over at the other unit and noticed that the back end was completely smashed in. I told Art, "No wonder they can't transport."

But there would be much more to the story.

We jumped out and grabbed our gurney. As we rounded the back of our unit I noticed, about 25 yards ahead of us, another crew—not Mary and Jerry—carrying a patient on a backboard toward us. They were nearly running with the patient and I thought for sure that they had a serious trauma. As they got close I realized that it was Steve and Robert. They had a frantic and hurried look in their eyes. I ran up to them with the gurney and told them, "We are good to go. Put the patient on our gurney and we will get out of here." The general rule in EMS is that the last unit in is usually the first unit out.

But both Steve and Robert told me firmly, "No, he's going with us."

I admit I was taken aback at first and a little irritated. "Guy's," I said, "just put him on our gurney and we will go."

Again they repeated, "He's going with us."

I finally realized that I was not going to win this fight and came up to the head of the backboard to help them carry the patient. I could see that the patient was in severe pain and that his legs had been severely damaged in the accident–they were completely busted and rotated around. There was no mistaking it was bad. As I got near the head my eyes also caught a glimpse of the patient's muddy and ragged shoulder patch. On it was an Emergency Medical Service Authority (EMSA) patch. Our patch. The patient was one of our own.

It was Jerry.

I felt a lump develop in my throat. I knew Jerry. He was one of my original trainers.

Apparently, a semi had blown through the warnings and hit Jerry just as he was bending down to put a patient, a victim of the original accident, into the ambulance. The impact missed Mary, but jerked the gurney out of her arms. I understand now that the impact caught Jerry and somehow threw him up and over, onto the side of the road. The gurney was thrown end over end with the patient on it. The patient remained on the gurney.

It is hard to explain just how hard the impact was, but the unit was smashed to halfway through the box. The unit was pushed greater than 25 feet on the impact.

I also understood why Steve and Robert wanted to take Jerry. Robert was Jerry's former long-time partner and good friend. Jerry was taken to

Saint Francis' Trauma center. He would survive and eventually return to work the streets a year later. He had numerous reconstructive surgeries and therapy.

The patient on the gurney? He was originally going because he'd had some back pain after being rearended on the highway. Now his wrist was broken and he had a concussion, but he too survived the impact. Funny, but due to his concussion and condition I had no idea what was wrong with him at first (in the commotion no one could tell me) and he couldn't remember, so I got the bright idea to ask one of the Oklahoma Highway patrolmen. He told me that he believed that our patient had hit Jerry. I didn't know any better and when the patient asked me for the twentieth time, "What happened?" I told him what the patrolman told me. I remember him asking me if it was really true and hollering, "No, tell me that's not true."

Hey, I didn't know. I was very respectful and treated my patient well, but since they both went to Saint Francis, I worried about having the two in the same emergency room. Obviously it wouldn't matter.

Ironically, that same week we had just received our new spider straps for the gurneys. They had a four-point harness instead of the regular three-piece straps. Amazingly I believe that that is what held the patient to the gurney. He never came off of it even thought all witnesses said that it rolled end over end.

They were both very fortunate. I had the opportunity to work with Jerry after that. I believe he was just a little bit mellower–not different–just mellower.

I think I would be too.

~ BE CAREFUL WHAT YOU WISH FOR ~

It was my last day as a full-time medic. I had accepted a position with Rogers State University and would be leaving the streets for a full-time academic position. I worked with Shane on this day. I liked Shane and we really had a good time together, so it made it alright for my last day.

Earlier, as we sat on post, I told Shane, "In all the time I was here, I never ran a call in Leonard." Leonard was our deepest response area to the south of Tulsa. It was a tiny town with fewer people than street signs. I'd heard some calls go out there, but none of them were mine.

Until my last day.

In the early evening we received a call to make run south of Tulsa. It was on the highway just outside of Bixby, and on the way to Leonard. I was finally making a run to Leonard. But unfortunately it was at the expense of two others.

The dispatch report said that we had two people hit by a car on the highway. I expected it to be bad and of course, it was.

As we pulled up we immediately saw two people on the ground about 20 feet from each other. A crowd of firemen and bystanders surrounded them. A large semi truck was parked on the side in front of a trail of dark skid marks. There was a dent in the hood about 2 feet in. I would later find out it was from one of the patients.

I jumped out and quickly triaged both patients. One was conscious and one was unconscious. They were both in bad shape so I decided to take the one who was unconscious, while my partner took the other patient. We immediately called for the Lifelight helicopter.

My patient was a large middle-aged man who had been riding his bicycle with the other man. For some reason bystanders told me they turned right in front of the semi that was travelling at high speed. Now, he was barely breathing and unconscious. I quickly intubated him and began breathing for him. I also put an IV line also. It was obvious he was going downhill fast.

The Lifelight medic and nurse came over as soon as their chopper landed and began assisting me. The nurse stood at the head and assessed the patient about the time the patient's heart stopped beating. We started CPR. We stuck a needle in his chest to help a collapsed lung. Nothing seemed to help. I told the Lifelight nurse that I was going to turn the patient over to him and take the second patient. I told him that I suspected that the patient had a hemothorax (blood in his lung) and a possible back injury. The nurse asked me, "Do want the other helicopter?"

"I don't think they can get here faster than we can load and go with the other patient," I told him.

"I can have them here in three minutes," he told me confidently.

"You have five," I said, knowing it will take me at least five minutes to load the second patient and get moving.

I walked over to Shane and the Bixby fireman as they readied the patient for transport. I had already checked the patient and felt he had a bad lung also, plus a back injury. I am sure there were probably some fractures in there too. I checked him again and found that his breathing had gotten worse. "We'd better get going with him," I told my colleagues.

As soon as we took him over to our unit the other helicopter was landing. Just in time. We loaded him on the chopper and I later found out he did have a hemothorax. He survived, but our original patient didn't make it.

And I wish I'd never run a call in Leonard

~ A MAN'S SOUL ~

Every EMS worker has that drive to help another. Usually that drive is due to a desire to see another happy. Sometimes that desire is due to pride. Whatever the reason we usually want so much to be able to help another and to save a life. Unfortunately all lives cannot be saved.

Phil and I rolled up on a possible DOA. It was at a low-income apartment complex on the West Side of Tulsa. We usually had a police escort when we responded here, as there were some inherent dangers we ran into at times, but this morning we didn't need one. We didn't need one because there was already a whole plethora of Tulsa Police Officers on scene. I wasn't there to save anyone, but to confirm what was already known—that the patient was dead.

I made my way through the crowd with my cardiac monitor. Tape had been put up and the officers were on edge. It was an obvious murder scene. I tiptoed into the front room, trying not to upset any evidence and was directed by the officers to a spot on the floor beside the couch. There lay the crumpled up body of a 12-year-old girl. She had been murdered during the night; stabbed brutally time and time again by a 14-year-old neighborhood boy who had wanted something she refused to give. There was no way to save her.

So I did my duty. I confirmed her death and wrote my report, but I hated this. I hated it more that someone was still around to have to feel the pain and sorrow. I looked around, but the only people in the apartment were the police officers and myself. I saw no family. Sadly, I was relieved that I didn't have to be the one to tell them. That is one of the hardest things to ever have to say. And children make it especially hard. But I didn't have to say a word to anyone this time.

And then I walked outside to leave. In the police car directly in front of the door I noticed someone in the passenger seat. He sat up as I walked out and looked right at me. I saw his eyes. They perked up for a second and then dropped back deep into their sockets. I hate the eyes sometimes; they *are* a window to a man's soul. And his soul was hurting. He wanted me to help. I was his last hope. His only hope.

But I walked away.

And I didn't have to say a word.

~ ANGELS ~

When you're a new medic it seems as if you can't wait to run on the auto accident. They just seem so exciting. Don't misunderstand me, it's not the idea of seeing someone else hurt or in pain, but it's more the incredible force behind one and the intrigue of "rescuing" someone. Reality is, we really don't see very many "bad" accidents compared to the common, "I 'd better go to the hospital with you just to get checked out"–even though the patient denies any compliant. They get very mundane and routine. Boring if you ask me.

As we pulled up to this scene Joe and I knew it was just another "routine" accident. We could tell from a distance as both drivers were already out of the cars and giving information to the Tulsa Police Officer on scene. One of the cars only had a driver, but the second car, which had been rearended at a stoplight, had an infant in a car seat in the front and two young boys in the back seat.

We parked in front of the scene and got out of the unit to do our standard, "Is everyone alright?"

Both drivers waved to me and said they were fine. I peeked into the car where the children still sat and checked on the little infant. The baby seemed just fine and was securely restrained. One of the Tulsa firemen had already checked on her and said she was fine when their engine had got there a few minutes before us. I then looked into the back seat and saw the two little boys. They were the same age, cousins I was told, and both said they didn't hurt when asked. The larger, stouter boy in the back was whimpering a little, but I initially attributed it to being scared.

About that time, the fireman who had originally checked them out, walked over and told me, "I think you had better check on the bigger boy. Something just doesn't seem right. Feel his head."

So I listened to what he had to say. I trusted the firemen in Tulsa. While at that time they played a first responder role, they were a very valuable ally to us at the Emergency Medical Service Authority (EMSA). I asked him what he meant and he told me that, "something felt funny on his head."

I climbed into the back seat. On the left side of the boy's head was an indentation, more of a depression, about a half-dollar size. He said he didn't hurt at all.

I tactfully now had to approach Mom. The fireman stayed in the car to hold the boy's head still so he would not move it. "Mom," I asked her softly, "Can I talk to you for a moment?" She acted a little perturbed that I would interrupt her while she spoke to the officer, but she looked at me. "Does your boy have any health problems?" I asked. She replied no.

I then asked her if he had any problems with his head, like you know, any holes? She chuckled, then said "no." I then explained to her the importance of the situation without trying to panic her. She didn't seem concerned in the least bit; after all, there was not even a dent in either car. *Literally no dent at all.* She told me that she would take him to her doctor when she finished with the police report. I had to talk her into letting me take him in the ambulance. She finally agreed, but followed us in her car—it was still driveable.

We put the boy on a backboard, secured his neck down, and then left the scene. Thankfully we only had two miles to get to Saint Francis so the transport would not be a long one. As we started out the boy was talking clear, had stopped crying, and denied feeling any pain. He seemed comfortable.

But things change quickly, especially in children. Shortly after we had pulled into traffic the boy started with some strange chewing motions with his mouth. I wasn't sure exactly why, but I did know that it was very abnormal. He also got quieter. When I him asked he still told me that he was "OK", but I could tell that things were changing. By the time we got to the ER, he was hardly talking to me. The chewing motion had now progressed into a focalized seizure and I knew the boy was in trouble.

We pulled up and hurried the boy into the ER, straight to a trauma bed. No sooner had I lifted him over then he started with projectile vomiting. The nurse and I quickly flipped him to his side so he would not choke on his vomit. She grabbed the suction and cleaned him out. Then he started with a full seizure. He was now in grave danger.

It turns out that the boy had a depressed skull fracture from the impact. He was in surgery a short time later and I understand that he survived—if he would have gone with mom and not straight to the hospital he may not have. But what impact caused the fracture? Surely not the simple car accident, remember there was not even a dent. So what was it?

I would find out later that it was his cousin who had caused the fracture. They had hit heads in the impact.

But more importantly was the fireman who checked the little boy out. Had I been there first, I doubt that I would have checked out the boy so thoroughly. Not because I was lazy, but because there really wasn't any reason to. At least there didn't *appear* to be a reason. That boy may have died if it wasn't for the alertness of that fireman.

I called him later and asked him just what it was that made him palpate that little boy's scalp, when there really wasn't a reason to. He said he didn't know, he just did. I am glad he did. There's a little boy who's glad that he did too.

I wish I could explain why things like that happen, but I can't. I have a theory though. *Someone told that fireman over his shoulder to check the little boy out.*

The problem was, no one could see him or her as they told him.

~ HIDDEN SURPRISES ~

For some reason Phil was a magnet for strange and bizarre calls. Everytime I worked with him it was something new and strange. Today was no different. We rolled to the very west of Tulsa to an area called "Town west". The call came in as a child struck by a car.

Both Phil and I had children and I think he was a lot like me and didn't really want to make a run like this. But Phil was a true professional and a great partner and he, like me, knew we had a duty to do. And someone needed our help.

As we pulled up to the scene we realized that we had beat the fire department's first responders. Some bystanders directed us to a spot on the side of the road where a young lady sat Indian style on the ground. We pulled up and parked the unit in front of her. From a distance I could see that she was moving and breathing. I relaxed. I also didn't see a child at the scene. That's always good news.

As Phil and I began asking her questions she told us that she was all right. She didn't act too concerned or worried. We commented to her that the report said that a child was involved.

And then she surprised us.

She had on a large shirt that she had drawn over her knees as if she was cold. Initially neither Phil nor I thought anything of it, but when we told the young lady about the report of a child she lifted her shirt up.

Underneath it was the child.

But he was moving and breathing and awake. That is always a good sign. And then we saw the tire tracks across his abdomen. And it hurt him when we touched it.

I immediately had Phil call for the helicopter. We had a decent transport time and heavy traffic on a torn up highway. I couldn't tell how bad the child might be hurt. It turns out that he was hurt, but would be all right.

Momma told us that her boy had unbuckled his seatbelt and opened the door to the pickup opposite her. So she let go of the wheel to grab him, but they both fell out of the truck. The truck then ran directly over the boy. She grabbed him and put him in her shirt. Why she didn't think it was important to tell us about the boy at first is beyond me, but not until we asked did she lift her shirt and reveal the boy.

Maybe she just likes surprises.

I don't.

~ A Faithful Following ~

The volunteer Keystone Fire Department was already on scene. They had responded as soon as the call came in. When you volunteer in your home area, someone on the squad usually knows the patient. And it was a Saturday, so all the volunteers were at home ready to respond. Upon our arrival we had quite a crowd. And someone knew the patient.

There was also a party going on for a little granddaughter, so the crowd was made even larger. The patient was an older man, who, after laying down a few hours earlier because, according to family, "he didn't feel well," was now on the floor, barely conscious. It became very obvious to me about 2 seconds through the door that he was having a stroke.

And it was a bad one.

I knew that by the time I could stabilize him and get him out the door we would have an hour transport. And unfortunately, time is so very critical in a stroke of this nature. So I decided to call the helicopter. Yet they wouldn't get here for another 15 minutes. So I went to work.

We took his vitals and checked his EKG. I started an IV and checked his blood sugar. It was normal so I knew that we didn't have a diabetic patient. Yet he continued to slip. He couldn't even open his eyes now. I couldn't get him to respond to us at all.

I wanted to help him, but I knew deep in my heart that this gentleman was on his last leg. He was dying and I felt so helpless. It doesn't matter how long you do this; death of another is never a welcome sight. At least not under these circumstances.

The helicopter landed and we quickly took him down the hill to where they were waiting on the now closed down highway. They took over care

79

for us and transported him to the hospital. I would later find out that he died that day.

Oh, I forgot to mention something. They were having the birthday party for the girl to keep her from getting too upset. They wanted to keep things as normal as possible. You see there had been another death that same morning. Someone in the family had died suddenly and they thought the party would help everyone cope better since it was already planned. Probably a good idea if you ask me. They seemed like a close family. And I am sure they missed their grandmother.

The wife of the stroke victim.

They died on the same day.

~ Last Day ~

I was leaving Tulsa to head back to school. 8 years and 3 children later (to bring our total to 4) I was actually leaving. I really couldn't believe it, but it was happening. I didn't want to admit it to anyone, but I knew I would miss this place.

I decided to work my last day with Heath, a former student and a good friend. We had talked about working together forever, but we just couldn't seem to hook up. Until today.

I figured that my last day would be a simple day, one that wouldn't require me to work too hard. After all, I considered myself a hard worker all these years. I tried doing alot to advance the cause of paramedicine and promote the service I worked for. I made some great friends, and I am sure a few enemies, during my career there. I tried hard to set a good example, especially for the new medics. I had trained three of the current supervisors. Yep, I'd like to think I had somewhat of a "legacy" there in Tulsa.

At least I deserved a nice quiet last shift.

Yea right. By now you know where I am going with this.

I should have suspected something early on when Heath and I were called to a house on the North side of Tulsa. An elderly neighbor reported to her visiting daughter that she hadn't seen her middle-aged neighbor for a few days. That and his papers had been piling up outside his house. She told her daughter that the neighbor was in ill health and she was concerned.

So the daughter went to investigate.

It's not something she'll ever forget. Going to the side door she found it unlocked. Upon entering into the house she made her way to the back room where she found him. On the bed, crossways, with a gun in his hand. He'd shot himself. He'd been down for a few days so there was nothing we could do for him, but pronounce him dead. He had no family and the note he left reflected that he was upset about having prostate cancer. So he ended it.

That should have been enough for us that day. I do not now and never have liked suicides. They leave an ugly pall hanging in the air. It's a feeling I cannot put into words, but one I never wish to feel again.

Later that day we responded to Berryhill, a small city to the west of Tulsa. They had a fire department with only one fireman on duty. If he was lucky he would get a contingent of volunteers to help him, but he wasn't always lucky. And today was a weekday, so he had to respond alone.

The call was in a run down mobile home off of a bumpy gravel road. We had reports that a man was down inside the trailer. Not necessarily a big deal, except that it had been 100 degrees the whole week with incredible humidity. We had recently experienced a rash of heat related emergencies and anytime a call came in like this it alerted us to the fact that we could have another one. We were also required to call in to our public relations officer and report any heat emergencies we ran on. Apparently there had been a quite of few calls to the PR officer lately.

And we were about to give him another one.

As we walked up to the mobile home and toward the stairs leading to the open front door, I could see the Berryhill fireman inside, on the carpet near the front door. He was kneeling over the patient who was next to the door.

The first thing I noticed, even before I actually made it through the door, was the oppressive heat and the smell—a mixture of urine and feces and vomit and dried sweat. Not a good smell if you ask me, but our patient needed us so we had to put that aside and do our job.

We got in the front door to find the patient on the floor. It looked like he had tried to get to the door to get some relief from the heat. He had no air conditioner. He did have a fan in the room, but with that high of heat in a virtual tin box, all it does is bring the warm air to you. Next to the patient was an electric wheelchair. Apparently, to complicate matters even more, he was also wheelchair bound. Poor guy couldn't even get out if he wanted to.

The Berryhill fireman was doing a wonderful job taking care of the patient. Covered in sweat and overheating himself, he had the patient on oxygen, had assessed him, and was prepared to give us a full report upon our arrival. The stench and the heat were unbearable in the room, which was unkempt in it's own right. I don't know how he did it, but he did an excellent job.

The patient was awake, but not responsive to us. That was a very bad sign. He was not sweating at this point. Another sign of severe heat stroke. But there was more. He had defecated on himself, urinated on himself, vomited on himself, and worst of all he had lain on his arm all night. It had already withered and he could not use it. On his chest where the arm sat was a large purple indentation about 3 inches deep.

We knew that we had to get him out of the trailer fast. At this point there is no guarantee he would make it anyway. Situations like this can lead to stroke, heart trouble, and kidney failure. He would no doubt have a long road ahead no matter what we do. But he deserved every chance we could give him.

I searched his house real quick for medications. He had one bottle–from 1989. I could find no record of medical history. There was no family. The neighbors didn't know anything about him. I felt blind. Nevertheless we had to get him to the hospital now. But it wouldn't be easy getting him outside. He weighed about 300 pounds and it took us a long time to get him onto the gurney and outside. It is one thing to pick someone up when they have normal muscular tone, but he was a flaccid as wet sheet.

I had found a little bit of ice in his freezer and wrapped it in some old towels to put it around his forehead. I put ice packs in his groin, and armpits to cool him. I put the IV fluid in a bucket of ice and ran that into him to help cool him off.

And then we drove.

For the first time that I can remember, after having worked there for 8 years, I gagged in the back of the truck. I felt so bad for the patient, but the stench was so strong that I gagged again and again. I thought I had a stomach of stone. I didn't lose it, but it was close. I put a protective mask on, put oxygen on myself, and turned the vent on high, but it was a tough ride. A very tough ride.

The patient remained the same enroute to the ER, but at the hospital he began to recover. He would make it. It felt good to really help someone on my last day. Sometimes it felt like we never really help anyone, so it was rewarding.

And now my career in Tulsa as a paramedic was over.

But I worked for it.

AFTERWORD

I realize that some of this reading may seem harsh and cold-hearted at times, especially to those not of the medical community. I assure the reader that there was no intent to make light of the true events chronicled in this book. While life does gives us some funny moments, it also gives us some sad and heartbreaking moments. I hope the reader can sense the feelings I had during those difficult times. I never wanted to see someone die unnecessarily, but it does happen. And death and dying are a part of all of us. I acknowledge that there are times when it is a natural process and should be allowed to take its course. I hope I did my best to let those who left this life on my shift to leave with dignity.

This book began as a journal to document the experiences of my career that stuck most vivid in my memory. There were thousands of other runs made that touched me personally, but didn't make it to print for various reasons. I acknowledge that they were no less important.

This book was about *my* career. I apologize to my former partners, co-workers, and other colleagues who may have also been touched by these same incidents in ways other than what I felt. You were a part of all these experiences. I never did it alone. I couldn't do it alone.

CONCLUSIONS

I feel so blessed to have been able to experience the things I have. It has not been an easy career, but it has been worth it. I am often amazed at the things I have witnessed, for good or for bad. I have seen the best of life, and the worst. I have watched others go through deep dark trials, and I myself have experienced my own. But I tell my patients one thing when they express to me their worries and fears, "The Lord must love you very much to try you so hard." I believe that no matter what we go through in this life we are in his hands. If our hearts and attitudes are in the right place, trials and tribulations only serve to make us stronger–if we let them. I know he watches over us.

I have met thousands of interesting people; people of different cultures, of different religions, and of different backgrounds. I believe that this has helped me learn *how* to love. It takes effort to see through the exterior and look to the heart of another. But deep down we all beat the same. Love *is* the answer. I believe it is *love* that truly heals another, not the medicine. Medicine cures often enough, but it usually doesn't heal. It takes love.

For all those who may someday consider a career in medicine, take the time to learn how to love another. I have heard others spoken of many times with the words, "His (or her) patient rapport stinks, but he knows his stuff." If your patient rapport is no good, than, in my opinion, you don't "know your stuff". I believe that your personal interaction with your patient is the *most* important factor.

In conclusion I thank once again all those wonderful partners who taught me and helped me, and served with me. I know I wasn't always the easiest partner to work with. For all those I may have offended over the years I offer my sincere apology. I usually meant well, but all to often my mouth got ahead of my brain and I spoke without thinking. I assure you I had the patient's best interest in my mind, even if I made a wrong decision.

And I thank all my patients. I owe you more than you'll ever know.

ABOUT THE AUTHOR

From his early days at Southland Ambulance in Anaheim, California to his later career in Tulsa, Oklahoma, Dale J Bingham has been a career member of the EMS community. During this time period He served in the management positions of Field Training Officer and Field Operations Supervisor.

The author has a B.S. in Health Services. For five years he served as a faculty member at Rogers State University in the Health Science Department, teaching all levels of EMS training. He has earned national honors in "Who's who of American Teachers (2000) and has given lectures nationally. He is an accomplished and published writer in both fiction and non-fiction.

He is currently a student at the Graduate School at the University of Utah. He is part of the Department of Family Practice Medicine, preparing to become a Physician Assistant.

LaVergne, TN USA
07 February 2011
215644LV00002B/2/A

9 780595 205929